Introduction to the American Legal System

Third Edition

By

Enika H. Schulze
P. Michael Jung
Rebecca P. Adams

Fifth Printing

Pearson Publications Company
Dallas, Texas

ISBN 0-929563-14-X

FOREWORD

The purpose of this book is to provide a comprehensive overview of the American legal system for the beginning student or beginning paralegal. The book explains basic legal concepts in a concise, easy-to-grasp way not readily available in current literature. Important concepts are highlighted for ease of comprehension.

An extensive glossary has been added to this edition to help the reader review and cross-reference, and the chapter on legal ethics received significant updating.

This book provides a general overview of the structure of the legal system, the criminal justice system, and the federal courts. It includes specific concepts and examples in the substantive areas of:

- torts
- contracts
- real property
- wills and intestate succession.

A chapter on legal research is included to orient the novice on issues of the law, legal material, and techniques of legal research.

Introduction to the American Legal System is also a popular study guide for the certificate examination offered by the National Association of Legal Assistants.

ACKNOWLEDGMENTS

The authors wish to express their appreciation to the Honorable Patrick E. Higginbotham, Judge of the United States Court of Appeals for the Fifth Circuit, whose continual insistence upon high standards and quality performance was the impetus for this project.

Appreciation is also extended to Walter E. Steele, Jr., Associate Dean for Clinical Education, Southern Methodist University School of Law, for his guidance in the early stages of this project.

Appreciation for revisions in this edition is expressed to Susan R. Patterson and Frances B. Whiteside, whose wording and attention to detail are superb.

We also thank Nancy Doherty, U.S. District Clerk for the Northern District of Texas, and her staff for providing important updates on the federal courts.

The Publisher

PREFACE

"The authors have done a superb job of providing a comprehensive and detailed description of the complex American legal system, written in a style that permits even beginning students of the legal system to understand the subject matter thoroughly. This volume will be a very valuable reference handbook to those whose livelihood is earned in American courts."

George R. Poehner, Former Chairman
Standing Committee on Legal Assistants
State Bar of Texas

"As a straight-forward description of the judicial process from beginning to end it is almost ideal for the person who is new to the court system.

. . .The book is arranged so that even the complete novice can grasp the basic ideas . . . [The authors] comment on the public's criticism, and then attempt to explain why a particular procedure or law is necessary in order to guarantee citizens their constitutional rights. This frank approach allows readers to look at the material in an intelligent manner, making their own judgments about the law's merits and faults."

Legal Information Alert

TABLE OF CONTENTS

CHAPTER I

GENERAL INTRODUCTION TO THE LEGAL SYSTEM

Basic Legal Concepts and Terminology.

1. Sources of American Law.

Modern American jurisprudence finds its origins in the small towns and villages of England. There, judges resolved disputes by making decisions that were based on custom, common sense, and fairness. These decisions, although at first not recorded, became part of an ancient tradition known as the **common law.**

As the common law developed, so did the principle of **stare decisis** or **precedent**. When a court made a decision based upon the facts of the case before it, that decision provided guidance for other courts faced with similar sets of facts. Gradually, the courts developed the policy that a decision of a court was binding on that court and on other courts of equal or lower rank when the same or a similar issue arose in the future. The reason for this policy was simple: people functioning in a society needed to know the rules so they could conduct themselves accordingly. They needed to know that a particular decision was the law, would remain the law, and would not be changed the next time a court was faced with the same issue.

In England, although the common law was the primary source of legal rules and principles, statutes gradually played an increasingly important role. **A statute** is an act of a legislative body that may be a prohibition, a command, or a declaration. The meaning of the various statutes was not always clear, however; nor was it always obvious that a statute was applicable to a particular set of facts. Thus, courts assumed the responsibility of construing statutes and applying them to various fact situations.

In the United States today, the common law, statutory law, and the principle of stare decisis form the backbone of our legal system. The courts of our nation, in resolving disputes or interpreting statutes, are guided by the decisions that other courts have made in the past when faced with the same or similar issues. These decisions, unlike those of the ancient English courts, are recorded and presented in law books so that lawyers, legal scholars, and judges may refer to them and study them whenever they need guidance.

2. Substance v. Procedure.

The rules that are the heart of our system of justice, whether they are legislative enactments or a part of the common law handed down by judges, are rules of **substantive law**. They state the rights and duties of individuals and the circumstances in which a court will grant one person redress against another.[1] Courts frequently are asked to resolve a question of substantive law. In some cases, they may have to determine the meaning of a particular statute. If there is no statute that applies to the facts before it, a court may have to decide what the common law rule should be in that sort of a case. If the rule has already been established by stare decisis, courts may have to determine whether the facts of that case fit the rule.

Courts reach these decisions by studying existing rules of substantive law and by relying on principles of justice and common sense. These rules of substantive law are very different from rules of **procedure**. The rules of procedure establish the step-by-step mechanics that people bringing or defending a lawsuit or criminal prosecution must follow. Each state establishes its own procedure, as do the federal courts. These procedures are the means by which people:

- gain access to the courts;
- conduct themselves during preparation for trial;
- conduct themselves during the trial itself;
- enforce the judgment of a court, once that judgment has been entered.[2]

Rules of procedure are very important. Their goal is to impose order on a dispute so that it will be resolved correctly, fairly, and quickly. They provide the method by which each party presents his or her story to the court in the way that is most conducive to a fair decision. Rules of procedure focus the dispute on only the relevant issues, thereby saving time and protecting litigants from prejudicial, immaterial evidence. They also give to the parties the means of discovering their opponent's position. Such discovery tools prevent unfair surprise; they also enable parties to present to the court a more complete story so that the court can better understand the truth. In federal courts, the procedural rules are known as the Federal Rules of Civil Procedure and the Federal Rules of Criminal Procedure.

3. Civil v. Criminal.

There are two basic types of disputes: civil and criminal. In a criminal case, the state or federal government brings an action against an individual to punish the individual for breaking one of their laws. A civil case is different. A person brings a lawsuit seeking some sort of redress for an injury the person claims to have suffered. The person may be an individual, a corporation, or sometimes even the state. The redress that the person seeks is usually in the form of money. The person asks the court to order an opponent to pay monetary compensation for the wrong that the opponent caused. For example, a person who loses an arm in an auto accident cannot ask the court to provide a new arm. One can, however, ask the court to require the person who caused the accident to pay monetary compensation for that arm. Of course, the problem with this system is that it is practically impossible to put a dollar value on something as priceless as an arm. How much money is an arm worth? or a person's health? or life? Although we cannot really put a price tag on things such as these, we can compensate the victim for certain specific losses. Thus, the person who caused the accident can be required to pay to the victim, among other things, whatever the victim's medical bills were or will be in the future, and whatever income the victim has lost or will lose as a result of the accident.

The Court.

The primary function of the court is the orderly resolution of disputes. These disputes may be between two private citizens, between a private citizen and the state or federal government, or even between two states. In later chapters we will explore in detail how the courts perform this vital task of mediating. First, however, we will examine several important characteristics of the courts that will give us a perspective on their role in our society.

1. The Judiciary and the Separation of Powers.

In the United States the judicial branch is one of the three branches of government. The other two branches are the executive (the President, or in the various states, the governor) and the legislative. Under the federal as well as the state constitutions, each branch acts as a check on the other two, ensuring that no one branch becomes overly powerful. The legislature, for example, has the power to enact laws. This power is not absolute, however. If the President or governor opposes a particular law, he or she may veto it. Similarly, the courts have the authority to check power of the other branches. Thus, a court may rule that a particular law that the legislature passed and the executive signed is unconstitutional. Such a law is void and has no force or effect.

2. The Judiciary and Federalism.

Just as there are a federal government and fifty different state governments, so is there a system of federal courts and fifty different state courts. Whereas the federal constitution created the federal courts, the different state constitutions created the state courts. In general, the federal and state courts function independently of each other. Although certain types of cases may be tried in a federal as well as in a state court, many cases may only be tried in state courts, and many others may only be tried in federal courts.

As a general proposition (although there are exceptions), the federal courts cannot interfere with or contradict the actions of a state court, and vice versa. Thus, if a person does not like a decision received in a federal court, that person cannot go to a state court and try the case a second time in the hopes of obtaining a more favorable ruling.

3. Courts as Protectors of the Individual and the Oppressed.

The courts play the important role of standing between the government and the individual and affording protection to the individual. They make certain that a person accused of a crime is not deprived of rights and receives a fair trial. Courts also insure that the majority of our citizens does not infringe on the rights of the minority. Legislators who tend to vote the majority views of their constituents may be unresponsive to minority groups who may espouse unpopular causes. The courts must be certain the majority, acting through the legislatures, does not deprive the unpopular minority of the rights to which everyone in this country is entitled. The decisions of the Supreme Court, for example, on abortion, desegregation, and prayer in public schools came about after legislatures failed to resolve these politically unpopular issues through legislative action.

In theory, the federal courts are more likely than state courts to make these unpopular decisions that protect the rights of the individual and of minorities more frequently than state courts. In recent years, however, state courts have been more responsive than the federal courts to civil rights claims, a reversal of the pattern in the 1960s and 1970s. This new trend may be due to a growing conservatism on the federal bench coupled with increasing public support for minority rights. One very important reason for this phenomenon is that in many states the state judges are elected for a term and then must face reelection, whereas all federal judges are appointed to their posts and serve for life. The federal judge, however, may make a ruling in favor of an unpopular group or individual and not run the risk of losing his or her job in the next election. The elected judge, however, is more prone to being influenced by popular opinion and, as a result, may protect the unpopular minority or the person accused of a crime less zealously than the appointed judge.

These two methods of selecting judges reflect two sharply differing views about democracy. Although the elected judge has the power to find that a law infringes on the rights of an individual or a minority, to declare that law unconstitutional and thus to cast aside the popular will, that judge is ultimately answerable to the majority, for the judge must ask the majority for reelection. This system of government may reflect the belief that the majority, which has ultimate control, will not infringe on the rights of the minority. Alternatively, it also may be based on the theory that even though the majority may sometimes infringe on the rights of the individual or the minority, such majority control is nonetheless the best method of governing a nation.

A system in which the executive nominates a judge with the advice and consent of the legislature reflects a different philosophy of government. The appointed judge who makes an unpopular decision need not fear public outrage, because he or she does not depend on the majority for reelection. If the appointed judge declares a law unconstitutional, he or she is answerable to no one except the judges who sit on a higher court within that judge's judicial system. This system reflects the view that the majority will not protect the rights of the minority, that the rights of that minority should be preserved, and that the duty of protecting those rights should be in the hands of persons who do not owe their jobs directly to the voters.

4. Courts as Passive Arbiters.

The judicial branch, unlike the legislative or executive, is passive. Whereas a legislature has the power to conceive of and enact laws, the courts may not institute lawsuits. A court may only take action after a party has come to it seeking the resolution of a dispute. Even then, because our courts function according to the adversary process, courts remain essentially passive. Under the adversary process, the court does not reach a decision until both sides have had the opportunity to present their evidence and arguments. Through this process of hearing the most thorough evidentiary presentations and best possible arguments that each side can muster, a court is best able to discern the truth and to do justice.

5. The Judge.

The judge, who is the chief officer of a court, is the settler of disputes. In fulfilling this responsibility, the judge must perform two main tasks. First, the judge -- or, if the parties request it, a jury -- must determine the facts. Naturally, in a heated dispute, there will be sharp disagreements as to what actually happened. In a controversy over who is ultimately responsible for damages suffered as a result of a traffic collision, for example, witnesses who were at the scene of the accident may give varying testimony on such fact issues as whether the light was green or red, whether the defendant gave a proper turn signal, or whether the plaintiff was speeding. Additional complications arise when the physical evidence conflicts with the statements made by the witnesses. These are all issues of fact that the judge or jury must resolve.

The judge performs his or her second major task by applying the law to the facts to determine who should prevail. In a simple traffic collision case, if either the judge or the jury finds that the defendant ran a red light, the judge must decide whether, under the law, the defendant was obligated to stop at that light. When the judge renders a decision, such findings are reduced to a written document called a **judgment**, which puts an end to the dispute. The judge's order is not irreversible, however, until both parties have exhausted their rights to appeal to a higher court. The judgment has the full power of the government behind it, and the sheriff or marshal will carry it out by force if necessary.

TERMS TO KNOW

common law
stare decisis
precedent
statute
substantive law
procedure
judgment

FOOTNOTES

1. R. Field and B. Kaplan, *Materials for a Basic Course in Civil Procedure* 2 (1973).
2. *Id* at 3.

CHAPTER II

THE CRIMINAL JUSTICE SYSTEM

Introduction.

A **crime** is an action that offends the morality of a society and that a society has determined it will not tolerate. The **criminal justice system** is that system which a society evolves to handle those who commit crimes. The term "criminal justice system" applies to the entire process from commission of a crime to punishment. This system necessarily reflects the values of its society, not just in the conduct that it punishes, but also in the way that it treats the accused and the criminal.

Systems that are characterized by strict enforcement of the laws, by a rapid determination of the guilt of the accused, and by harsh punishment are frequently found in nations that grant defendants few rights. When compared to the United States, these nations are more likely to regiment their citizens, restrict their behavior, and interfere in their private lives.

Since its beginning, the United States has regarded itself as a different sort of society. Many of the people who settled the new nation left their homelands to be free from what they considered to be excessive government intrusion. They recognized the importance of restricting the power of government and protecting the individual citizen from the power of the state. Consequently, the states passed the Bill of Rights, which became the first ten amendments to the Constitution. Those amendments, which grant the person accused of a crime many vital rights, form the foundation of the nation's criminal justice system.

Our criminal justice system today, however, is the subject of much criticism. Many members of the public believe that they are not safe, that crime is rampant, that the police are not effective in catching the wrongdoer and that the system -- lawyers, judges and prosecutors -- is excessively lenient.

The crime-fearing public that criticizes the courts in this way overlooks a crucial fact: the problems that lie at the root of crime are not lenient judges or clever lawyers, but instead are such things as poverty, poor education, and the breakdown of the family structure. These are conditions that the criminal justice system cannot and should not be expected to correct.

The criminal justice system already has an extraordinarily difficult task. It must strike a delicate balance among the sometimes competing interests in protecting the accused from the tyrannical intrusion of the state, vindicating the public morality by punishing the wrongdoer, and enforcing the criminal laws in such a way as to protect society from future crimes. This is indeed a formidable task. To the outsider, the criminal justice system that has evolved to tackle this difficult job may appear to be a confusing maze. There are numerous courts and several sets of criminal laws.

Cases in federal court involve the alleged violation of federal criminal laws and cases in state court, the alleged violation of state criminal laws. Both federal and state laws divide criminal conduct into two categories: **misdemeanors** and **felonies**. Misdemeanors range from traffic violations to such offenses as theft of a small amount of money. A felony is a major crime for which the maximum penalty may be a fine or imprisonment or both. Felonies include such offenses as homicide, arson, rape, robbery, burglary, and grand larceny.

Federal and most state courts are divided into three levels. First, and at the lowest level, is the trial court. In that court, the actual trial is conducted and the accused is found guilty or not guilty. At the next level are the appeals courts, and usually there are several such courts. Finally, each state has a supreme court, and the federal system has the **United States Supreme Court**.

Within the state criminal justice system, there are generally several different trial courts. The cases that these courts may hear depend upon their **jurisdiction**. Jurisdiction is a term that refers to the power or authority of a court to hear and decide a particular kind of case. The lowest level courts, for example, often have jurisdiction only over such crimes as traffic violations, criminal trespass, and public intoxication. Other courts hear only more serious misdemeanors, such as petit larceny, while the highest level of trial courts hears only felony cases.

In 1967, the President's Commission on Law Enforcement and Administration of Justice issued a Task Force Report on the Courts.[1] The Commission inquired into the effectiveness and fairness of America's criminal courts and found that the aspects of the criminal court system most in need of reform were the lower criminal courts in urban areas. Because most crimes are committed in the cities, these courts handle the majority of all cases that are tried. Literally millions of arrested persons first appear before these courts, either for trial of misdemeanor or petty offenses or for preliminary proceedings in more serious cases. Of the nation's criminal cases, the vast majority are heard in the urban lower courts. These courts often operate with meager facilities, with the least trained personnel, and with the most oppressive workload. Practices by judges, prosecutors, and defense counsel that would be condemned in the higher courts may still be found in these courts.

Judgeships in such lower courts are often elective offices. Pressures from "friends" and interest groups and the practice of accepting campaign contributions from lawyers make impartiality difficult. In those cities where judges are appointed and where the salaries are adequate, the quality of justice is significantly higher. Able and experienced lawyers often find appointment to a municipal judgeship very desirable. Not infrequently, hundreds of applications will be received for one such position. Some qualified appointed municipal court judges may find their quality of justice hampered, however, because their courts are not **courts of record**, which means the proceedings are not recorded by a court reporter. When a case is appealed from such a court, the case must be retried by a higher court. The appeal is then ***de novo***, that is, the case is tried again. A serious problem with a *de novo* appeal is that by the time the appeal is heard, witnesses may no longer be available, and the memory of those witnesses who are available may have faded. On the other hand, in a court of record, when a case is appealed, the court reporter records everything that was said in the trial court. This record is submitted to the appeals court, along with all the documents filed in the case. The appeals court then renders a decision based on the lower court record.

Improvements at the lower court level will have the most far-reaching effects. If the criminal justice system does not provide the best possible service at this level, we may cast an unnecessary shadow over the entire legal system. The millions of individuals who have contact only with these lower courts form opinions based on their experiences that, at best, reduce their respect for the system, and at worst, result in hardening of antisocial attitudes.

The Rights of the Accused.

Although many courts *are* inefficient and render justice which is not always fair, in some cases what may be *perceived* as inefficient or unfair may in fact be due to the constant tension that exists between the public's demand for strict and quick administration of justice on the one hand and protections for the rights of defendants on the other. These protections stem primarily from Supreme Court interpretations of the United States Constitution.

Many of the basic concepts about criminal justice are stated in the first ten amendments to the United States Constitution, the Bill of Rights. All rights and privileges of the criminal defendant that the Bill of Rights contains may be referred to collectively as **procedural due process**. Although the Bill of Rights was originally intended as a limitation on the federal government, the Court has now applied almost all of the Bill of Rights to the states.

The law of criminal justice in the United States is a curious amalgamation of state and federal law. Although each state is free to define what is a crime, and to create its own court system and criminal procedure for processing the crimes through its courts, the state cannot go beyond certain limits set in the United States Constitution. These limits are set out in the Bill of Rights.

The Fourth Amendment states: "The right of the people to be secure in their persons, houses, papers and effects against unreasonable searches and seizures shall not be violated, and no Warrants shall issue, but upon probable cause . . ." The Supreme Court has interpreted the Fourth Amendment to mean that one is free from search unless the police have probable cause to believe that there is contraband or evidence of the suspected crime at the place to be searched. Suspicion of a crime is inadequate for search or arrest: **probable cause**, that quantum of evidence that leads a reasonable person to believe that guilt is more than a possibility, is the essential element. Evidence that is obtained in violation of the standards set out in the Fourth Amendment must be excluded from court. This rule is known as the **exclusionary rule.**[2] The rule however, does not prevent police from seizing evidence of unsuspected crimes during a legal search and using search evidence to bring additional charges.[3]

Among the Fifth Amendment's limitations on criminal justice is a provision that all federal felony charges be brought in the form of a **grand jury indictment**. The states are not constitutionally required to have grand juries, but about half of them do so. A **grand jury** is an official body of citizens brought together to decide whether a person accused of a crime should be officially charged. If the grand jury decides to officially charge, the charge is called an indictment. The purpose of the grand jury is to provide a barrier between the state -- law enforcement agencies -- and the individual.

The Fifth Amendment protects a defendant from double jeopardy -- being tried twice for the same offense. Once a person is found innocent of a charge, the prosecution cannot bring the same charge again. Nevertheless, the Supreme Court has recently ruled that a defendant can be charged with a different offense based on conduct for which he or she has already been prosecuted.[4]

Perhaps the most famous clause in the Fifth Amendment provides that a person shall not be compelled, in a criminal case, to be a witness against himself or herself. This is called the **privilege against self-incrimination.** The defendant does not have to prove that he or she did not commit a crime. The defendant does not even have to talk about it or take the witness stand. Instead, the prosecutor has the burden of proving that the defendant is guilty.

The United States Supreme Court has extended this privilege against self-incrimination to apply also to preliminary questioning by a police officer. Because this rule was established in a case called *Miranda v. Arizona*,[5] the rights enumerated in that case are called **Miranda warnings**. In general, prior to any questioning, a person must be advised that he or she has the right to remain silent, that any statement the person does make may be used against the person, and that the person has the right to the presence of an attorney, to be provided by the government if the accused cannot afford an attorney. Like evidence obtained in violation of the Fourth Amendment, evidence obtained in violation of *Miranda* under the Fifth Amendment must be excluded from court under the exclusionary rule.

The Sixth Amendment provides that in all but the most minor criminal cases the trial must be by an impartial jury. The defendant may, however, waive his or her right to trial by jury and be tried instead by the judge. Another clause in the Sixth Amendment states that the defendant has the right "to be informed of the nature and cause of the accusation." An **indictment** or other charging instrument must contain precise technical language concerning the nature and cause of the accusation, because the defendant may only be tried on those offenses listed in the charging instrument. Therefore evidence pertaining to any other offenses is usually not admissible during trial.

The Sixth Amendment also states that "in all criminal prosecutions the accused shall enjoy the right . . . to be confronted with the witnesses against him." This clause gives a criminal defendant the right to be present in the courtroom at every stage of the trial. It also ensures the defendant the right to cross-examine those who testify against him or her.

Finally, the Sixth Amendment gives a defendant the right to the assistance of counsel for his or her defense. Although anyone who can afford a lawyer may hire one at any stage of a criminal proceeding, the Supreme Court has interpreted this clause to mean that even those who cannot afford an attorney have the right to one. The Court has held that if a defendant is indigent, the judge must appoint an attorney to represent the defendant. Lying at the heart of this rule is the Court's realization that without an attorney, a defendant's chances of having a fair trial are slim. The Supreme Court has also ruled that the criminal defendant has the right to effective assistance of counsel and that if a defendant is convicted and the defense attorney's omissions or failures were sufficiently egregious, the conviction is not valid.

The right to be represented by counsel is not limited to defendants who are tried for serious offenses. The Supreme Court has ruled that "no person may be imprisoned for any offense; whether classified as petty, misdemeanor or felony, unless he was represented by counsel at his trial."[6] Therefore, if a person could go to prison -- even for a day -- as punishment for the offense with which he or she is charged, such person has the right to counsel. If, however, the maximum penalty is only a fine, the accused does not have the right to a court-appointed lawyer.

The Eighth Amendment forbids "cruel and unusual punishment." Courts have had great difficulty defining this elusive term. After many years of varying interpretations, it has come to mean punishment characterized by the unnecessary and wanton infliction of pain that is out of proportion to the crime. For example, in 1977 the Supreme Court ruled that the death penalty is out of proportion to the crime of rape where no life is taken.[7] In recent years the Eighth Amendment has been raised frequently by prisoners filing law suits in which they complain that prison conditions are so appalling as to constitute cruel and unusual punishment. The Eighth Amendment also prohibits "excessive fines." In 1993, the Supreme Court ruled that forfeitures of property owned by defendants convicted under federal drug laws are subject to the Eighth Amendment test against excessive fines.[8]

The Lawyers.

1. Prosecution.

The role of the prosecutor in a criminal case is complicated. The prosecutor's most visible responsibility is as a representative of the government prosecuting a defendant in a particular criminal case. Because of the limited manpower and financial resources available to prosecutors, not all of the many cases presented to a prosecutor will be prosecuted. Prosecutors have considerable discretion about which cases they prosecute, and a prosecutor will not take a case to trial unless he or she believes that a conviction is both warranted and achievable. To reach this conclusion, the prosecutor must rely on more evidence than may eventually be produced at trial. Like all attorneys, prosecutors want to win the cases they try and, unlike the defendant, they generally cannot appeal cases they lose. Therefore, they will usually prosecute their strongest cases. Some cases, however, will be prosecuted regardless of their strength

-- for example, cases against defendants believed to be guilty of previous offenses and believed to be likely to commit future ones unless prevented from doing so.

Contrary to common belief, the responsibility of the prosecutor is not merely to convict. The American Bar Association Code of Professional Responsibility requires the prosecutor to "seek justice." This special duty exists because:

- the prosecutor represents the sovereign and therefore should use restraint in the discretionary exercise of governmental powers, such as in the selection of cases to prosecute;

- during trial the prosecutor is not only an advocate but he or she also may make decisions normally made by an individual client, and those affecting the public interest should be fair to all; and

- in our system of criminal justice the accused is to be given the benefit of all reasonable doubts.

The prosecutorial decision to charge is based on complex factors. The most important is the seriousness of the crime, followed by the strength of the evidence. Also important is the criminal record of the accused. Obviously, if the crime is serious, the evidence strong and the defendant a repeat offender, the prosecutor will bring charges. Conversely, if the accused is a first-time offender and acted in response to provocation from an undesirable victim, the prosecutor may bring a lesser charge, or even none at all.[9]

Political pressures also bear upon a prosecutor's decision to charge. Political pressures are greatest in the state courts where prosecutors are elected. They or their assistants may be persuaded not to prosecute politically unpopular cases. For instance, cases against community leaders or children of community leaders may never see the courtroom. Generally speaking, the more articulate or wealthy a defendant, the greater will be public sympathy toward him or her, which may compel a prosecutor to charge a lesser crime or recommend a more lenient punishment.[10]

Federal courts are less political. United States attorneys are appointed by the President with the advice and consent of the Senate and are less immune to local political pressure. Staff attorney positions at the Department of Justice, the Department of Labor and other departments with prosecutorial responsibilities are highly competitive and generally go to individuals with solid law school records, rather than those with merely political connections.

2. Defense Counsel.

Prosecutors and defense counsel play significantly different roles. Their ethical responsibilities vary accordingly. Defense counsel's obligations center around the constitutional right to counsel, the constitutional right against self-incrimination, the presumption of innocence and burden of proof, and confidentiality between attorney and client.[11]

Contrary to public belief, criminal defense lawyers make up only a small percentage of the practicing bar. Most lawyers advise clients about their business affairs. Few handle litigation, and the majority of those handle only civil litigation. Many lawyers handling criminal cases are not criminal lawyers at all but have been appointed by the court to represent indigent defendants. The vast majority of the people convicted of serious crimes are indigent.[12]

Some states and most large urban areas have a public defender system. The quality of public defenders varies greatly from district to district. Public defenders are greatly overworked. They simply have too few resources and too many clients to defend. Most cases handled by public defenders end in plea bargains, so that scarce resources can be allocated to those defendants with meritorious cases.[13]

The first question a criminal defense lawyer must ask is whether to represent a particular client. The American Bar Association says:

> A lawyer is under no obligation to act as adviser or advocate for every person who may wish to become his client; but in furtherance of the objective of the bar to make legal services available, a lawyer should not lightly decline proffered employment. The fulfillment of this objective requires acceptance by a lawyer of his share of tendered employment which may be unattractive both to him and the bar generally.[14]
>
> However, a lawyer should decline employment if the intensity of his personal feelings as distinguished from community attitudes may impair his effective representation of a prospective client.[15]

When a lawyer is appointed by the court to represent an indigent defendant, the ABA Code of Professional Responsibility imposes stricter standards. Only for compelling reasons should a lawyer decline such representation. "Compelling reasons do not include such factors as the repugnance of the subject matter of the proceeding, the identity or position of a person involved in the case, the belief of the lawyer that the defendant in a criminal proceeding is guilty . . . ."[16]

A lawyer should not withdraw from a case merely because the lawyer discovers that his or her client is guilty. In order for an adversary system to work properly, it is necessary that the defendant have a spokesperson in court, just as the prosecutor is the spokesperson for society. Defense counsel should present the best defense he or she can in the best interest of the client. Defense counsel may decide to present nothing but try to put the prosecutor's case in the worst possible light. The prosecutor has the obligation to present the evidence and to prove the defendant guilty.

The Sixth Amendment, guaranteeing the right to assistance of counsel, would be rendered meaningless if members of the bar did not have a corresponding duty to represent all those who need representation, regardless of guilt or innocence and regardless of how distasteful the alleged crime may be. The late Edward Bennett Williams, an experienced criminal trial lawyer, explained that:

> Defending an unpopular client is an open invitation to be widely misunderstood . . . Every time I have assumed the defense of a case in which the crime charged is a heinous one, or the defendant is a social or political outcast, the criticism has come.[17]

Unfortunately, many Americans have the bad habit of associating the lawyer with the crime the lawyer is defending, rather than regarding the lawyer as an officer of the court who is the agent of the accused. This view reflects a misconception of the lawyer's role: as proposed ABA Model Rule of Professional Conduct 1.2(b) states, "(a) lawyer's representation of a client, including representation by appointment, does not constitute an endorsement of the client's political, economic, social or moral views or activities."

Since lawyers representing unpopular clients run the risk of identification with their clients in the public mind, they have a particularly heavy responsibility. The question that should be asked is not whether a lawyer can defend an unpopular client but, rather, what the lawyer can legally and ethically do for his or her client. The clash between two opposing sides presents the most effective way of determining the truth, and so the attorney's function in an adversary system is to represent the client to the best of his or her ability.

To be able to represent fully the interest of the client, an attorney must maintain uninhibited communication with the client. The ABA Standard Relating to the Defense Function (3.2) states that as soon as practicable, the lawyer should seek to determine all relevant facts known to the accused. "In so doing, the lawyer should probe for all legally relevant information without seeking to influence the direction of the client's responses." The ABA Standard further indicates that it is unprofessional conduct for any lawyer to instruct the client or to intimate to the client in any way that the client should not be candid in revealing facts so as to afford the lawyer free reign to take action.

Pretrial Process.

The criminal justice process consists of several different stages. At each stage fewer accused individuals will be involved. As individuals move through the stages of the pretrial process, their numbers decrease. The process may be viewed as a pyramid. On the bottom are the number of individuals arrested; on a higher level, those charged with an offense; and, on the very top, the very few who are convicted. We will now examine the various stages of the criminal justice process to determine how and where the individuals drop from the system.

1. Investigation.

The criminal justice process begins when the police are led to believe that a crime has been committed. Investigation may be initiated in several ways:

- when police observe a crime being committed or observe a person acting suspiciously.
- when a victim or other affected party reports that a crime was committed.
- when the police decide to look for specific criminal activity that they believe is occurring or about to occur.

The latter may result from accumulated police experience or from a tip from an informer.

The police may use such investigating techniques as examination of physical evidence left at the scene of a crime, interrogation of suspiciously acting persons, search of persons or premises, electronic eavesdropping, and various undercover activities.

2. Arrest.

If upon investigation the police officer decides that enough evidence exists to believe with probable cause that a crime has been committed by a particular person, he or she may make an arrest, taking a person into custody and, usually, transporting the person arrested to the police station where the person is "booked." Most arrests are made without warrants and are based on witnessing of offenses being committed, on reports of offenses having been committed, or on belief that persons are acting suspiciously.

The officer may use such force as is necessary to detain and hold a felony suspect, including deadly force in some situations and in some jurisdictions. In some jurisdictions, arrests for misdemeanors cannot be made without a warrant unless the officer witnessed the commission of the misdemeanor. In other words, since only minor crimes are involved, the right of an officer to make a warrantless arrest is limited. For minor violations, instead of taking the suspect into immediate physical custody, the officer may issue a **citation**, which is an order to appear before a judge at a later date. The officer may use reasonable force, but not deadly force, to detain and hold the suspect in a misdemeanor.

At bookings for felonies and some serious misdemeanors, the suspect is ordinarily fingerprinted. These prints are sent to the FBI to determine if the suspect is wanted elsewhere. As discussed earlier, in any interrogation, the police must give the suspect his or her Miranda warnings, which advise the suspect of his or her rights to remain silent and to have immediate assistance of counsel.

3. Bail.

Soon after the suspect is arrested, he or she is brought before a magistrate for consideration of bail. The usual form of release pending trial is for the defendant to post a **bail bond**. A bail bond is a legal document containing a promise of the defendant to appear for the trial of the case or to forfeit a sum of money. The sum of money can be guaranteed by a deposit of cash (**cash bond**) or the guarantee of another to pay the amount of the bond if the defendant fails to appear (**surety bond**). Bail bonds, especially when they involve a minor offense or misdemeanor, are sometimes also referred to as **appearance bonds**. The magistrate determines whether the defendant is bondable and the amount of the bond. Such a determination is based primarily on the defendant's prior record and the seriousness of the offense. These criteria are weighed to determine the defendant's likelihood of appearing for trial. Should a defendant have good "roots" in the community (local job, residence and family) and have no prior felony conviction, the defendant may be released on his or her **personal recognizance**. This simply means that the defendant agrees to appear at the trial without having to put up a sum of money to guarantee his or her appearance. In areas that have a **pretrial release program**, a pretrial release officer checks out the defendant's background and, if the officer determines the defendant to be a good risk, recommends approval of a pretrial release bond. The defendant pays a small premium for such a bond and is released until trial.

4. Charging.

When bail is set, the evidence held by the police is forwarded to the prosecutor to determine whether to charge the suspect. If the prosecutor agrees with the police that there is probable cause to believe that a crime was committed and that the accused committed it, the prosecutor may decide to formalize the charge. In practice, only a fraction of the cases booked by the police are charged at the same offense level recommended by the prosecutor.[18]

One way to charge a suspect formally is to seek an **indictment** from a grand jury. Grand juries are available in about half the states and in the federal system, but only a few jurisdictions use the grand jury exclusively in bringing felony charges. The number of individuals on the grand jury varies from state to state. Grand jury proceedings are secret, with neither the defendant nor defense counsel present. The prosecutor appears before the jury, presents the case, and asks for an indictment. Members of the grand jury can ask any questions they wish and can subpoena witnesses to ask them any questions. They may vote to issue an indictment on the charge requested or on some other charge, or they may decide not to indict at all. Although in the majority of cases grand juries follow the prosecutor's request, they are designed to serve as a check on the power of a prosecutor to go forward with a prosection.[19]

An alternative to indictment by grand jury is by a charging document called an **information** or, sometimes, a **complaint**. This document is prepared by the prosecutor in lieu of going to the grand jury and generally occurs in misdemeanor cases. Complaints are usually presented at pretrial hearings where the judge can assess the evidence and decide whether or not to proceed with or dismiss a case for lack of probable cause.[20]

5. Arraignment.

After the indictment is returned or the information is filed, the defendant is brought into court where the prosecutor reads the charge. In some jurisdictions this appearance is called an

arraignment. After the charges are read, the defendant must plead to them. The defendant may plead to the charges as "guilty," "not guilty," or "***nolo contendere***" ("I will not contest it"). The latter plea may not be used in another case as proof that the defendant committed the act, although in all other respects it is a guilty plea.

Before accepting a plea of guilty, the judge must inquire of the defendant if the defendant understands what he or she is doing and must determine that the defendant voluntarily pleads. The judge must also warn the defendant of the possible sentencing consequences and determine that the defendant is competent. Many judges will also inquire into the factual basis for the plea. In federal court the judge also usually advises the defendant that he or she has the right to plead "not guilty" and be tried by a jury, the right to confront and cross-examine witnesses against the defendant, and the right not to be compelled to self-incrimination. If the court accepts a "guilty" plea, there will be no trial and the next stage will be sentencing.

6. Plea Bargaining.

In most jurisdictions, the prosecutor and defense counsel may engage in **plea bargaining**. This may take place at any stage of the proceeding prior to completion of trial; it may even occur during trial. Plea bargaining involves negotiation between prosecutor and defense to enter a guilty plea in exchange for the reduction of charges or some other benefit to the defendant. The judge should not participate in such discussions, but the judge should require the disclosure of the agreement in open court at the time the plea is offered. A defense lawyer has the responsibility of fully advising his or her client about whether a particular plea bargain should be accepted.

Plea bargains were approved by the United States Supreme Court in the case of *Santobello v. New York.*[21] Plea bargains are entered into because attorneys concern themselves with the likely outcome of cases. The inquiry they make is usually what the jury will do, rather than what it should do. If a defense counsel anticipates an adverse jury verdict, he or she may decide a guilty plea to lesser charges is in the client's best interest. Prosecutors are interested in obtaining plea bargains, usually because they have more cases than they can possibly try. Defense attorneys on the other hand will plea a case because they believe that a trial will not achieve a better result for the defendant and may, in fact, result in a heavier sentence.[22]

Another consideration that enters into the plea bargain process is the fact that jails are unpleasant places. If a defendant pleads guilty, he or she is generally free to go until the day of sentencing. Therefore, a defendant who has not been able to make bail is highly motivated to plead guilty in order to expedite his or her release from jail. For those unable to make bail, the consolation is that pretrial jail time may reduce the eventual sentence.

7. Pretrial Motions.

Frequently, a defendant will plead "not guilty" in the initial stages of the process, and after pretrial motions are decided, change such plea to "guilty." A **motion** is a request to the court that it act in a certain way. For instance, a motion may request the court to dismiss the case, or to move the case to another jurisdiction, or perhaps to order that the government produce certain evidence for the defendant to examine before trial. Some of the more common pretrial motions are:

a. **Motion for Discovery and Inspection**. To prepare for trial, attorneys on both sides must gather information relevant to the case. This process of gathering information is called **discovery**. In most jurisdictions, the government must permit the defendant to inspect and copy relevant written or recorded statements made by the defendant that are within the possession of the government. A copy of a prior criminal record, if any, and other documents in the custody of the government that are material to the preparation of the defense should be provided to the defense attorney. A defendant will file a motion for discovery and inspection if the government fails to provide requested discovery.

b. **Motion for Bill of Particulars**. A motion for bill of particulars asks the court to order the government to file a formal document giving details of the time, place, and manner in which the alleged crime was committed.

c. **Motion for Change of Venue**. A defendant is generally tried in the district in which the crime is alleged to have been committed. If there appears to be such prejudice that the defendant could not obtain a fair trial in that district, the court may grant a motion for change of **venue** (the geographical location in which the case is tried).

d. **Motion to Sever**. In a case where two defendants are being tried together, one of them may feel that he or she will be prejudiced by the bad reputation of the other, by the strength of the evidence against the other, or by the confession of the other. If the court grants a motion to sever, the two will be tried separately.

e. **Motions to Suppress Evidence or to Dismiss the Indictment**. These motions are frequently based on alleged violations of a defendant's constitutional rights. For example, because all courts have interpreted the Constitution to require that the indictment precisely set forth the nature of the charges against the defendant, some defense counsel may file motions to dismiss the indictment on the ground that it is not sufficiently specific. Many motions are filed claiming that evidence the prosecution intends to introduce at trial was seized in an illegal search in violation of the Fourth Amendment. If the court finds that the evidence was illegally seized, it must suppress the evidence. This means that the evidence may not be introduced at the trial. If the evidence is crucial to the prosecution's case, the prosecutor may decide to abandon the case when the motion to suppress is granted.

The public often criticizes courts for granting motions to dismiss or to suppress evidence, and claims that judges are letting defendants go free for things that are "minor technicalities." This attitude often is a product of ignorance about the nature and the importance of the constitutional rights at stake. Although a wrongdoer might have his or her case dismissed because a police officer did not have probable cause to arrest and search the individual, it would be much more unfortunate if police officers could arrest or search anyone without probable cause to believe that such person committed a crime. The constitutional probable cause requirement intentionally curbs police power so that innocent citizens cannot be harassed, arrested, or jailed as in a totalitarian state. Thus, the occasional freeing of a criminal can be a small price to pay to preserve fundamental constitutional rights for all of us.

Trial.

After the case survives the motion stage of the trial process and if the defendant persists in his or her "not guilty" plea, the case will be tried. The Sixth Amendment guarantees a defendant a trial by jury in all cases where imprisonment is a possible outcome. The defendant may, however, waive this right with the approval of the court and the consent of the government. In that event, the case will be tried by the judge.

1. Jury Selection.

A jury trial begins with the selection of a **jury panel**. The panel usually consists of about thirty to forty members, depending upon the number of defendants involved in the case, chosen by some random process. In both federal and state courts, jurors who have reached this stage will have certain characteristics in common. They will be:

- citizens of the United States and residents of the district for a specified term.
- able to read, write, speak and understand English; and
- able to fill out the juror questionnaire form.

They will be without mental or physical infirmities rendering service unsatisfactory and without charges pending or convictions for a serious crime. Judges who check the qualifications of prospective jurors excuse those who do not meet these criteria. Because jurors are often selected from voter lists, jurors are not often a representative cross section of the community. Young people are less likely to be registered voters than are older people. Poor people are much less likely to vote than the middle class. Professionals, such as doctors, lawyers, and teachers, often get excused. A jury panel is thus not a random cross section of the community.

The next step in the process is **voir dire** examination of the jury panel. Voir dire literally means to "speak the truth," and comes from Old French. The objective of the voir dire examination is to secure a fair and impartial jury. During this examination the prospective jurors are questioned by the judge or by the attorneys about their background, family, employment, and other aspects of their lives that may be considered relevant.

Although the stated objective is to select impartial jurors, in reality attorneys try to get jurors that will "vote" for their clients. In the process of questioning jurors, the lawyers try to influence and persuade them, presenting themselves as being the "good guys." Prosecutors and defense counsel naturally look for different types of jurors. Defendants prefer jurors who are like themselves, while prosecutors seek jurors who are like the victim.[23]

The manner of jury selection varies greatly from state court to federal court and from judge to judge. In some state court systems, the attorneys ask the questions of prospective jurors. In addition to asking questions, state court prosecutors often explain the duties of jurors, define relevant terms, and question jurors about their attitudes on conviction, sentencing, and so on.

In federal court, the judge generally asks the questions although it is within the judge's discretion to allow the attorneys to do so (*Fed. R. Crim.* P. 24). In courts where the judge conducts the voir dire, attorneys may submit written questions they would like the judge to ask.

Parties on either side may ask that a member of the panel be excused if the examination indicates the panel member is not qualified to be a juror or that the panel member may be prejudiced. Such request is called a **challenge for cause**. The parties also have a right to a certain number of general challenges or strikes, called **preemptory challenges**, which may be exercised without giving any reason. It is not impermissible to eliminate a juror for any given trial due to race, gender, age, or any other classification. However, a defendant may be able to challenge a conviction successfully if it can be proved that the jurisdiction in which he or she was convicted systematically discriminates against classes of jurors, especially on the basis of race.

The stated objective of the voir dire examination is to find a jury that will make a fair decision. A defense counsel representing a particularly unappealing client may decide, however, to waive the jury and instead have a trial before the judge, expecting the judge to be more "fair" than a jury.

2. Staging the Trial.

After a jury has been selected, the jurors are seated in the jury box. An oath is administered to them by the court, requiring them to render a true verdict. The attorneys then make their opening remarks, informing the judge and the jury what they believe the evidence will show.

The trial itself is somewhat like a stage performance, with the judge and lawyers writing the script. The courtroom is usually arranged with the judge's bench in the front of the courtroom, the jury box on one side, the prosecutor's table closest to the jury box and the defendant's table farthest from the jury box. The government or state agent who had responsibility for investigating the case will sit with the prosecutor, and the defendant will sit with his or her counsel. Spectators may sit on the benches in the back of the courtroom behind the "bar." Although the courtroom is open to the public and anyone may come and go, the atmosphere is formal, particularly in federal court, and dress is required to be appropriate. In most courts, when the judge enters or leaves the courtroom, everyone must rise, and when addressing the judge, attorneys and clients must stand.

The lawyers generally try to create maximum impact and maximum drama. The criminal trial has a greater importance, however, than a drama. Beyond the public spectacle lies a fact-finding process bound by rules of evidence. The chief function of the judicial machinery is to ascertain the truth.

If the objective is to find the truth, what about the public's right to know the truth? The First Amendment guarantees the right to freedom of the press, but what if that freedom comes in conflict with the fact-finding mission of the judicial process? This conflict is obviously a serious one. Much has been written by justices of the Supreme Court and others weighing the relative importance of these two interests.

3. Publicity.

In cases that get newspaper coverage, the judge usually instructs the jury not to read any newspaper articles about the case. Jurors must make their decisions based on evidence presented in court, without influence from outside sources such as newspapers. Moreover, newspaper accounts are often inaccurate. Reporters are usually not lawyers, and their exposure to the legal system is often infrequent and haphazard. Discussions about whether to allow or not to allow certain evidence are often conducted in court after the jury has been excused or before the jury is brought into the courtroom. Certain information of interest to the general public may be excluded from a jury's consideration because it is unreliable and may mislead them or because the evidence is obtained in unauthorized ways. Perhaps the defendant has confessed, but the confession is not admissible. If such information is included in newspaper accounts, a very misleading interpretation could be drawn. Jurors must render a verdict based only on admissible evidence developed during the trial.

If newspaper reporters are allowed in the courtroom, should television cameramen also be allowed? In 1965, at a time when television equipment was bulky and obtrusive, the Supreme Court held that television coverage of a criminal trial was so physically disruptive that the defendant was denied due process of law. *Estes v. Texas*, 381 U.S. 532 (1965). In 1981, however, the Supreme Court, reviewing the advances in television technology made in recent years, explained that the *Estes* case did not establish a per se rule barring television coverage, but instead meant only that the particular television coverage in that case had deprived the defendant of his rights. *Chandler v. Florida*, 449 U.S. 560 (1981). The Court held that allowing television coverage was a matter for each state to decide, neither constitutionally required nor constitutionally prohibited. It left the door open for a defendant to show that television coverage had disrupted his or her particular trial, or had prejudiced his or her particular judge or jury, but refused to presume that this type of injury would occur in all cases.

Today, more than ten years after *Chandler*, television cameras are widely accepted in the courtroom, although usually within the discretion of the trial judge.

The American Bar Association's Code of Professional Responsibility restricts an attorney from revealing information to the press or to someone who may reasonably be expected to reveal it to the press. Only the following statements may be made:

- information in a public record;
- the fact that an investigation is in progress and the general scope of the investigation; and
- a request for assistance in apprehending a suspect.

An attorney may not make statements that could be expected to be disseminated to the press regarding a party's character, reputation or prior criminal record; the existence of a confession, admission, or statement by the accused or the failure of the accused to give the same; the performance or result of a test; the identity, testimony, or credibility of a prospective witness; or any opinions as to guilt or innocence of the accused or the merits of the case against the accused.

However, basic facts such as the name, age, residence, occupation, and family status of the accused, the nature of the charge, and the status of the judicial proceedings may be revealed. After completion of the trial, extrajudicial statements that might affect the imposition of sentence are prohibited. In cases where there has been too much pretrial publicity, the judge may grant a motion for change of venue, transferring the case to another area where the publicity may have been less. Of course, some cases have received national press attention, and the defendant cannot be given a fair trial anywhere. In that event, the defendant may get a trial that is only as "fair a trial as we can give him."[24]

4. Presenting Evidence.

The great majority of cases have no press interest at all. They proceed according to a more or less routine schedule. After the jury is seated and sworn, the charging instrument is read to the jury, and the defendant enters his or her plea. Then the prosecutor begins presentation of his or her case by calling the first prosecution witness to testify. Each witness will first be questioned by the prosecuting attorney. This process is called **direct examination**. Attorneys often try to question witnesses in such a way that the witness' answer will be to their greatest benefit. Documents that pertain to the witness' testimony may also be presented in evidence at that time. Such documents must be marked as **exhibits** and must carry exhibit numbers. All documents must be shown to the opposing counsel, the judge, and the jury. When the prosecuting attorney has completed interrogation of the witness, the defendant's attorney has an opportunity to ask that witness questions. This process is called **cross-examination**.

After the prosecutor has completed questioning all his or her witnesses and the defense counsel has cross-examined them, the prosecutor rests. Defense counsel may then start his or her case by calling the defense witnesses and presenting documents. If the defense counsel believes that the prosecutor has not proved the prosecutor's case, defense counsel may rest without putting on any witnesses. Or, the defense counsel may decide to call some witnesses but not to put the defendant on the stand. By law, the fact that the defendant does not testify may not be considered as evidence against the defendant. Any witnesses the defense does produce will be cross-examined by the prosecutor. The defense counsel's objective is to disprove the prosecutor's case and to discredit the prosecutor's witnesses or to establish some affirmative defense such as self-defense or insanity.

5. Jury Instructions.

At the conclusion of presentation of evidence, attorneys on both sides usually meet with the judge in chambers to determine what the judge's **jury charge** will be. Both sides may present specific instructions they wish the judge to make. Objections to instructions should be recorded by the court reporter.

In addition to the judge's instructions to the jury, the lawyers have an opportunity to present closing arguments to the jury. In their arguments, they will attempt to summarize the evidence and interpret to the jury what they believe the evidence showed. Each side will try to appear more believable than the other side. After both sides have presented closing arguments, the prosecutor, who has the burden of proof, has a final opportunity to argue. Closing arguments may be offered either before or after the judge instructs the jury, depending upon the local rule. In the judge's instructions, he or she will instruct the jury on the rules of law that they must follow and apply in arriving at a decision in the case. The judge will state that it is his or her duty to preside over the trial to determine what testimony and evidence is relevant under the law for their consideration and that they must follow his or her instructions. Some judges use standard jury instructions. Standard jury instructions in federal court include the following:

> . . . Upon retiring to the jury room you should first select one of your number to act as your foreman or forewoman who will preside over

> your deliberations and will be your spokesperson in court.
>
> . . . Any verdict must represent the considered judgment of each juror. In order to return a verdict, it is necessary that each jury agree thereto. In other words, your verdict must be unanimous.
>
> . . . It is your duty as jurors, to consult with one another, and to deliberate in an effort to reach agreement if you can do so without violence to individual judgment. Each of you must decide the case for yourself, but only after an impartial consideration of the evidence in the case with your fellow jurors. In the course of your deliberations, do not hesitate to reexamine your own views and change your opinion if convinced it is erroneous. But do not surrender your honest conviction as to the weight or effect of the evidence solely because of the opinion of your fellow jurors, or for the mere purpose of returning a verdict.
>
> Remember at all times, you are not partisans. You are judges -- judges of the facts. Your sole interest is to seek the truth from the evidence in the case.[25]

Standard jury instructions have been adopted by many trial courts in an effort to balance the sometimes conflicting objectives of maintaining jury instructions simple and intelligible for a lay audience and yet technically precise enough to pass an appellate court's scrutiny.[26] Whenever a case is appealed, the appellate court will examine the court reporter's transcript of the trial court proceedings, including instructions that were given to the jury. Errors in instruction may be cause for reversal of the trial court's decision.

A jury may deliberate as long as is necessary to reach a unanimous verdict. Some juries may reach a verdict in a couple of hours. Other juries deliberate for days or even weeks. On occasion, a jury will report that it is hopelessly deadlocked and unable to reach a verdict. This is called a **hung jury**. The judge then declares a mistrial, and the case may be tried again to a different jury before the same or a different judge.

In addition to the obvious service a jury performs in rendering a verdict, a jury serves another important function: that of bringing societal values into the courtroom. The jury, in effect, serves as a check upon the legislature and any unpopular laws it may have passed. Marijuana laws are unpopular in some areas, and juries bring in verdicts of innocence in marijuana cases in those areas. If juries continually fail to convict, they may force legislatures to change the laws. During the prohibition era, the legislature did exactly that.

Sentencing.

In some state courts, a jury that finds the defendant guilty may be sent back to the jury room to deliberate about the defendant's sentence. In other state courts and in the federal courts, the judge does the sentencing. In federal court, when a jury renders a guilty verdict, the judge usually sets a date for sentencing several weeks hence. During the interim, a United States Probation Officer will prepare a background investigation on the defendant. The result of this investigation is compiled in a document called a **presentence report**. A presentence report will also be prepared on defendants who have pled guilty and waived their right to trial. The presentence report includes the defendant's version of the event as well as the official version, personal and family data, the defendant's employment record, health and military history, the defendant's financial condition, and so forth. The report also includes the defendant's prior record, if any, and any charges against the defendant that may currently be pending. In the final paragraph of the report, the probation officer usually recommends a sentence which he or she believes appropriate in the case, within the legally established maximum and minimum for each offense. The judge may or may not follow this recommendation. Most judges will require defense counsel to examine the presentence report and review it with the defendant.

Many judges consider the task of sentencing a heavy burden. In spite of guidelines and recommendations from the prosecutor, at the state level, the weight of sentencing responsibility falls on the judge. At the federal level, newly promulgated sentencing guidelines have diluted judicial discretion in sentencing. Designed to insure greater uniformity of sentencing across the federal system, the guidelines have, some argue, replaced the power of the judge to determine a sentence with the power of a prosecutor to determine what severity of crime to charge.

A judge may begin his or her sentencing duty with the question: "What am I trying to do?"[27] **Deterrence**, **protection of the public**, **rehabilitation**, and **retribution** are objectives that have been asserted. One or more of this group of four objectives generally becomes the focus of the judge's consideration. If deterrence of similar crimes by potential new offenders is the judge's primary consideration, he or she may consider not only the type of sentence to best accomplish that function but also how that sentence will be communicated to potential offenders.

Deterrence is often the primary objective in white collar crimes. For more violent crimes, such as rape, protection of the public may be the primary consideration. Rehabilitation may be the most difficult objective, given the low level of achievement and educability of most prisoners.[28] Retribution is also a complicated objective. Historically it has been assumed that for every crime there would be retribution. Community guilt feelings or vengeance often played a part. United States Circuit Judge Patrick E. Higginbotham finds that the criminal sentence is "laced with release of community guilt feelings and atonement."[29]

In spite of the different objectives in sentencing, authorities seem to agree that if laws are to have any power, failure to obey the laws must be accompanied by punishment. In other words, a commitment to law as a specific form of government is already logically a commitment to the policy of punishing violators. The very concept of law itself embodies the concept of retributive punishment.[30]

The concept of sentencing is firmly rooted in society, and judges will continue to struggle with sentencing objectives and the types of sentences to impose. Although a judge has considerable latitude in the sentence he or she imposes, minimum and maximum sentences for types of offenses are fixed by law. The most common sentences are **probation** or a term of **imprisonment**. A combination of the two is referred to as a **split sentence**. Under a split sentence, the defendant serves a short term in prison, such as six months, and the balance of his or her time on probation. An alternative to imprisonment is the **suspended sentence** with a fixed term of probation. Whenever imposition of sentence is suspended and the defendant is placed on probation, and the defendant violates the terms of that probation, the judge may later sentence the defendant and impose a prison term if the judge considers the probation violation to be serious.

Another sentencing alternative is the **fine**. A fine may be imposed by itself, or in association with probation or, even, imprisonment. The money received from fines goes to the government. If the court orders the payment of restitution, the money goes to the victim. **Restitution** is frequently set as one of the conditions of probation. General conditions of probation include a requirement that the probationer report to the probation office on a regular basis, usually once a month, at which time the probation officer makes sure the probationer is employed and that his or her current address is known. Most felony probationers may not travel outside the state.

Defendants who are on probation are thus under continued supervision by the court, through its probation officers. Any time a probationer violates the terms of his or her probation, the probationer may be called before the court to determine if his or her probation should be revoked. Such a hearing is called a **probation revocation hearing**. Many probationers who have abused their probation privileges have found themselves in prison.

The philosophy and mechanics of sentencing are the subject of much ongoing debate. New proposals are continually being advanced in an effort to accommodate both the interests of society and those of the criminal defendant.

Appeal.

Individuals convicted of criminal offenses have the right to appeal their convictions. Those convicted in state courts can generally appeal through their state's supreme court. Likewise, those convicted in federal courts ultimately can seek a hearing before the Supreme Court. In most cases, appeals courts have discretion whether or not to hear an appeal based on some alleged error in the lower court's proceedings. State defendants have access to federal courts for the purpose of appealing only if they assert that the state failed to observe a federally-imposed procedural guarantee. These include (1) the right to a jury trial for serious offenses, (2) the assistance of counsel if a jail sentence may be imposed, (3) the privilege against self-incrimination, (4) that guilt be established beyond a reasonable doubt, (5) the right to refuse to take part in a police interrogation or to have an attorney present, and (6) freedom from racial and sexual discrimination.[31]

Many people think of the criminal justice system as the process by which a criminal defendant is tried in a courtroom before a jury. This chapter has illustrated the narrowness of that point of view: the process is an ongoing one, from the time a person arouses the suspicion of the police officer on the beat to the time the criminal has served out his or her imprisonment, parole, or probation. Many individuals enter the system only once, at the lowest level, and are never charged with or convicted of crime. Others pass through the entire length of the system time and time again, returning to a life of crime as soon as they gain their freedom. For this reason, the presumption of innocence, which is critical to our system of criminal justice, is often difficult to put into practice.

TERMS TO KNOW

crime
criminal justice system
misdemeanors
felon
United States Supreme Court
jurisdiction
court of record
de novo
procedural due process
probable cause
exclusionary rule
grand jury indictment
grand jury
privilege against self-incrimination
Miranda warnings
indictment
citation
bail bond
cash bond
surety bond
appearance bond
personal recognizance
pretrial release program
indictment
information
complaint
arraignment
nolo contendere
plea bargaining
motion
discovery
venue
voir dire examination
jury panel
challenge for cause
peremptory challenge
direct examination
cross examination
jury charge
hung jury
presentence report
deterrence
protection of the public
rehabilitation
retribution
probation
imprisonment
split sentence
suspended sentence
time
restriction
probation revocation hearing
sentencing guidelines

FOOTNOTES

1. The President's Commission on Law Enforcement and Administration of Justice, *Task Force Report: The Courts* (1967)
2. See *Mapp v. Ohio*, 367 U.S. 643 (1961).
3. See *Minnesota v. Dickerson*, 508 U.S. ___ (1993).
4. See *United States v. Dixon*, 509 U.S. ___ (1993).
5. 384 U.S. 436 (1966).
6. *Argersinger v. Hamlin*, 407 U.S. 25 (1972).
7. *Coker v. Georgia*, 433 U.S. 584 (1977).
8. See *Austin v. United States*, 509 U.S. ___ (1993).
9. J. Kaplan, *Criminal Justice: Cases and Materials* (1986) (cited as "*Cases*").
10. *Id.*
11. J. Kaplan, *Criminal Justice: Cases and Materials, Teacher's Manual* (1973).
12. J. Kaplan, *Cases, supra.*
13. *Id.*
14. ABA *Code of Professional Responsibility*, EC 2-26.
15. EC 2-30.
16. EC 2-29.
17. Glazer, *What Are the Limits of a Lawyer's Professional Conduct in Defending a Client*, 54 Fla. B.J. 2 (1976).
18. J. Kaplan, *Cases, supra.*
19. *Id.*
20. *Id.*
21. 404 U.S. 257 (1971).
22. J. Kaplan, *Cases, supra.*
23. J. Kaplan, *Cases supra.*
24. *Id.*
25. U.S. Fifth Circuit District Judges Association, *Pattern Jury Instructions, Criminal Cases* (1979).
26. ABA Commission on Standards of Judicial Administration, *Trial Courts* (1976).
27. Higginbotham, *The Philosophy of Sentencing*, 42 Tex. B.J. 497, 499 (1979).
28. J. Kaplan, *Cases, supra.*
29. Higginbotham.
30. Fingarette, *Law and Punishment*, 50 Proc. and Addresses Am Philosophical A. No.
31. J. Kaplan, *Cases, supra.*

CHAPTER III

SUBSTANTIVE CIVIL LAW

In contrast to criminal law, which regulates the conduct of individuals through the threat of fines and imprisonment, civil law defines the legal significance of public and private acts and regulates conduct through **injunctions** and the award of money damages.

The topics covered by substantive civil law are as varied as the conduct that the law attempts to regulate. Many types of civil law are created by statute. Federal statutes create liability for securities fraud, antitrust conspiracies, patent, trademark, and copyright infringement, and all types of federal taxes, to name a few categories. State statutes, such as statutes prohibiting deceptive trade practices, may also create civil liability. Statutes may also define the legal consequences of certain acts or conditions, such as statutes which provide for the distribution of the property of those who die without a will, or statutes which define the effectiveness of an unrecorded deed. Beyond the statutes passed by Congress and the state legislatures (and, of course, the administrative regulations adopted under those statutes) is the **common law**, which sets forth the standards of conduct applicable in most day-to-day situations and establishes the rules of liability in most civil lawsuits.

The remainder of this chapter will discuss four of the most fundamental areas of the common law: torts, contracts, the law of real property, and the law of wills and descent of property. This is not to say, of course, that a variety of other statutory and common law topics will not be relevant to the legal assistant. On the contrary, many legal assistants spend a great deal of their time working on complex litigation such as securities fraud matters. Nevertheless, an understanding of the basic principles of the fundamental areas of the common law is essential to an understanding of more complex areas of substantive civil law.

Torts.

A **tort** may be broadly defined as an act or omission to act which causes legal harm to another, committed under circumstances where the law imposes a duty to refrain from causing such harm. Although some torts, such as **fraud**, may be connected with a contractual relationship, the obligation to refrain from committing a tort is usually one imposed by law and not by any agreement between the parties.

Torts fall into three broad categories: intentional torts, such as **battery**; negligent torts; and so-called "**strict liability torts**," such as the marketing of an unreasonably dangerous product.

Apart from torts such as fraud, which will be discussed later, there are six principal intentional torts:

- assault
- battery
- false imprisonment
- intentional infliction of emotional distress
- trespass
- conversion.

Most of these torts are derived from the old English **writ of trespass**, which in medieval times was a quasi-criminal remedy for redress of a direct and usually intentional injury. As their label implies, each of these modern torts must be committed intentionally. This does not mean, however, that the person who commits the tort (referred to in legal parlance as the **tortfeasor**) must have wanted the resulting harm to occur; it is sufficient that the tortfeasor be aware that harm is substantially certain to occur. Thus, for example, someone who blows up a plane in order to kill one passenger has committed an intentional tort against all the passengers who are injured, even if he or she had no desire to harm any of the other passengers.

It is not necessary that the tortfeasor anticipate all of the harmful consequences that actually follow from the commission of the tort: he or she will be held liable for all results that are reasonably foreseeable. For example, a robber who clubs his or her victim, intending only to incapacitate the victim, but who "unintentionally" kills the victim, is liable for all the resulting harm. It is not even necessary that the tortfeasor intend that the harmed individual be the one to suffer harm: under the **doctrine of transferred intent**, the intent to harm one person is "transferred" to the person who was actually harmed. Thus if a tortfeasor attempts to strike A, but misses and instead strikes B, he or she has committed an intentional tort against B even if the tortfeasor had no intention to strike B.

Battery is defined as the harmful or offensive touching of another, such as striking another with one's fist. It is not necessary that the contact be directly with the victim's body; any harmful or offensive touching of the clothing, or of an object closely associated with the body, such as a plate held in the hand, is sufficient to constitute a battery. The harm need not be caused directly; thus one who digs a hole into which he or she knows his or her victim will fall is guilty of a battery. The contact need not be physically harmful, as any contact that a person of reasonable sensibilities would find offensive is a battery. It is not even necessary that the victim be aware of the contact at the time of its occurrence; hence someone who is kissed by a stranger while asleep has a valid claim for battery.

The tort of **assault** consists of placing someone in the apprehension of an immediate battery. The actual battery need not occur for there to be an assault; all that is necessary is that the victim reasonably expect that a battery is about to follow. A prime example would be raising one's fist to strike. Nor does "apprehension" refer to fear on the part of the victim: a ninety-pound weakling may assault a heavyweight prize fighter if the latter is led to expect that an immediate battery, that is, an immediate harmful or offensive touching, will occur. It is not necessary that a battery be actually physically possible. Hence pointing an unloaded gun at someone may constitute an assault if the victim does not know the gun is unloaded. The apprehension must be of an immediate battery: a threat to commit a battery in the future is not sufficient.

False imprisonment consists of restraining someone within a bounded area against that person's will: the tort commonly referred to as "false arrest" is a good example. It is not necessary that the victim be confined to a small area, but it is essential that the area be bounded. Thus, confining someone to a city would be false imprisonment, but preventing someone from entering a building would not. The restraint may be by actual physical force or may consist of the expressed or implied threat of physical force. The force or threat of force may be directed toward the victim, the victim's immediate family, or the victim's property. In cases where the restraint causes actual physical harm, the victim need not be aware of the restraint at the time; thus a sleeping person who is confined and suffers harm may recover for false imprisonment.

Finally, false imprisonment, like many other torts, may occur through an act or through a failure to act where there is a duty to act. Thus, for example, a jailer who fails to release a prisoner at the appropriate time is liable for false imprisonment.[1]

The **intentional infliction of emotional distress** is sometimes a tort. In order for recovery to be allowed, the defendant's conduct must be extreme and outrageous, transcending all bounds of common decency. Except in special situations, such as the conduct of a common transportation carrier or innkeeper toward a customer, or conduct directed toward a child or other person of special sensibilities, offensive or insulting language is not ordinarily sufficient to constitute the tort of intentional infliction of emotional distress.

In most cases, the severe emotional distress must result in physical consequences or symptoms before a recovery will be permitted. Under some limited circumstances, a person who causes another to witness an injury to a third party (usually a member of the victim's family) and thereby causes the victim to suffer severe emotional distress, will be held liable.[2]

The predecessor of most modern intentional torts is the tort of **trespass**. A trespass is an intentional interference with an individual's right to exclusive and complete possession of land or tangible goods. The right to possession of land includes the right to use a reasonable amount of airspace above the land as well as the space beneath the surface. Thus one may commit a trespass by throwing or shooting a projectile over someone's land or by mining underneath it.

In the case of trespass to land, it is not necessary to prove any physical damage in order to recover, while for trespass to physical objects (**chattels**) it is necessary to show damage to the chattel, injury to its owner, or deprivation of its use for a substantial period of time.

The law of **conversion** is complex and detailed. In sum, the *Second Restatement of Torts*, §222A, defines conversion as "an intentional exercise of dominion or control over a chattel which so seriously interferes with the right of another to control it that the actor may justly be required to pay the other the full value of the chattel."

By far the majority of modern tort lawsuits are not concerned with intentional torts, but with **negligence**. Negligence consists of four basic elements:

- a duty to conform to a certain standard, established by law
- a failure to meet the standard
- a cause-and-effect relationship between that failure and the resulting injury; and
- damages resulting from the injury.

All four of these elements must be present before there can be a recovery for negligence.

The standard of conduct established by law is expressed with reference to the conduct of a hypothetical "reasonable person of ordinary prudence, acting under the same or similar circumstances." Negligence consists of doing what a reasonable person would not do under the circumstances or of not doing what a reasonable person would do under the circumstances. Thus, it is no defense that the tortfeasor is as careful as he or she knows how to be if the tortfeasor does not exercise so-called "ordinary care."

One who is incapable of ordinary care due to insanity, mental deficiency, or simple stupidity is nonetheless liable for negligence if his or her actions do not measure up to this hypothetical standard. Only children are permitted a lesser standard: the conduct of a child is judged by the conduct of a typical child of the same age, intelligence, and experience. The ordinary rules of negligence are applicable in the case of alleged malpractice by professionals such as doctors, lawyers, accountants, architects, and the like. Thus, for example, a physician is liable if he or she does not conform to the standard of knowledge and skill of medical practitioners in good standing in the physician's community. This does not mean that the physician will be liable for any error of judgment: there is negligence only where the error is one that a competent practitioner would not make.

While general practitioners are governed by the standards of other general practitioners in the community, a specialist is held to the standard of others practicing the same specialty, and the comparison is not limited to those in his or her community. Except where the medical implications of the defendant's conduct are obvious to a layperson (such as where a surgeon mistakenly removes the wrong kidney), expert testimony is required to establish the appropriate medical standard of care. Liability for malpractice is not limited to direct negligence by the physician: the physician may also be liable where he or she fails to obtain the "informed consent" of the patient before performing a procedure. Malpractice liability is not limited to physicians: in this regard you may wish to review Wade, *Tort Liability of Paralegals and Lawyers Who Utilize Their Services.*[3]

Where a statute prohibits certain conduct, courts often hold that a violation of the statute is itself negligence. This doctrine is known as **negligence per se**. In order for a plaintiff to rely on negligence per se, the plaintiff must establish that he or she is a member of the class of people for whose benefit the statute was enacted and that the harm which he or she suffered is the kind of harm the statute was enacted to prevent. Thus, a motorist who is struck at night by a car that has no headlights may recover for negligence, since nighttime accidents were one of the evils that the headlight law was designed to prevent, and nighttime motorists were the group to be protected.[4] It is necessary, however, that the violation of the law play a part in causing the injury; thus one who is speeding is not automatically liable for any accidents that may occur, but only for those in which excessive speed played a part.

A specialized form of proof of negligence goes by the imposing name of ***res ipsa loquitur***. This phrase is Latin for "the thing speaks for itself." Where an accident occurs that is of a type that does not ordinarily take place in the absence of negligence, where the object or instrumentality that causes the accident was in the exclusive control of the defendant, and where the accident cannot have been due to any action of the plaintiff, the judge or jury is permitted to infer that the accident occurred as a result of the defendant's negligence. Thus, for example, in an old English case a barrel of flour fell out of the second floor of the defendant's warehouse and struck the plaintiff. Since such a circumstance does not ordinarily come about unless someone is negligent, since the barrel was in the exclusive control of the defendant, and since the plaintiff could not have been at fault, *res ipsa loquitur* was applied.[5]

In order for there to be liability for negligence, two types of **causation** must be present. These are commonly known as **causation in fact**, on the one hand, and "legal" or **proximate causation** on the other.

Causation in fact is relatively straightforward: the negligent conduct causes the resulting injury if the injury would not have occurred if the negligent conduct had not occurred. Where there are two or more causes for a single injury, as where fires negligently set by two individuals combine and burn down a house, a tortfeasor is liable if the tortfeasor's conduct was a substantial factor in causing the injury.

The concept of legal or proximate causation is harder to understand. The law does not impose liability for every injury that is caused in fact by tortious conduct, but only for those injuries that are sufficiently direct. Thus in a case where a ship was negligently moored, broke loose, floated downstream, struck another ship and caused it to break loose, following which the two ships struck a bridge and caused the bridge to collapse and dam up a river, flooding the land upstream, the tortfeasor was forced to pay for the flood damage, because such damage was regarded as sufficiently direct. But the tortfeasor was not liable for damages to the owner of a ship whose path was blocked by the collapsed bridge, because that injury was determined to be too remote.[6]

The problem of determining which injuries are sufficiently direct is one of the most difficult problems in tort law. A good rule of thumb is that a defendant will be held liable for all the injuries that the defendant might have reasonably foreseen would result from his or her conduct. If a second cause intervenes to produce the injuries, the defendant will be held liable if that cause was reasonably foreseeable, but not otherwise. Thus, if a roof falls in a high wind, the defendant may be liable if the high wind was reasonably foreseeable but will not be liable if the wind was stronger than might reasonably have been expected.[7]

Not all negligent actions or inactions that proximately cause injuries are the subject of tort liability. In addition to these elements, there must be a duty to act or not to act that is imposed by law. While one ordinarily has a duty to prevent harm to others, this is not always the case. For example, a person is ordinarily under no duty to save someone from a danger that the person has not created. While it may be morally reprehensible to stand by and watch someone suffer injury, one who does so is not liable for damages. If, however, aid is given, it must be given in a reasonable manner: one who begins to aid a person and then abandons the person may have caused others not to come to the person's assistance, while one who gives aid in a negligent manner may cause further injury.

The duty of a landowner with respect to dangerous conditions on his or her land is governed by special rules. A landowner is ordinarily not liable for injuries to someone outside the landowner's land as a result of dangerous natural conditions of the land, such as a rotten tree on the edge of the land which falls and injures a passerby.[8] The landowner is generally liable, however, for injuries caused by artificial conditions that the landowner negligently fails to correct.

In most states, persons on a defendant's land are divided into three categories for purposes of analyzing the landowner's duty toward them. First are those who are on the land without express or implied permission, that is, those who are **trespassers**. A landowner's sole duty to a trespasser is to refrain from "wilfully or wantonly" injuring the trespasser. Thus, observed trespassers must be warned of known dangerous conditions on the land, and the landowner must exercise reasonable care in avoiding injury to the trespasser from the landowner's active operations once the trespasser is discovered. There is ordinarily no duty, however, toward undiscovered trespassers, except to avoid wanton conduct in disregard of the danger to any trespasser who might be on the premises. Thus, for example, a landowner would not be liable if an undiscovered trespasser falls into a pit on the land, but the landowner might be liable if he or she shoots a gun recklessly without regard for whether there are any trespassers on the premises.

A special exception to this rule exists in the case of trespassing children and goes by the name of **attractive nuisance**. If the landowner knows or should know that children are likely to trespass but negligently allows an unreasonably dangerous condition to exist, which condition results in injury to trespassing children because they cannot learn of or appreciate the danger, the landowner will be held liable. Despite the name of this doctrine, it is not necessary that the child be "attracted" onto the premises by the dangerous condition; it is only necessary that the presence of children can be reasonably anticipated.

The second category of visitors on a defendant's land is that of **licensees**. Licensees are those persons who are on the land with permission and for a legitimate purpose but who are not there as ordinary members of the public or for a business purpose of the landowner. Common examples of licensees include members of the landowner's family and house or social guests. The duty of a landowner toward a licensee is one of ordinary care; in other words, the general negligence standard applies. This means that the landowner must exercise ordinary care to refrain from injuring the licensee and must warn a licensee of hidden dangers that he or she is likely to encounter.

The final category is that of **invitees**, those who are on land as members of the public or to further the business interests of the landowner. Examples include passengers in public conveyances or customers in a store. The term "invitee" is misleading: the fact that someone has received an invitation to come onto the land does not necessarily make that person an invitee. Social guests, discussed above, are a prime example. A person possesses the status of an invitee only so long as he or she remains on the property for the business purpose of the owner. Thus, a customer who loiters in a store for an unreasonable time after making a purchase, or who travels to areas of the store not open to the public, will lose invitee status. The owner owes a duty to an invitee to maintain premises in a reasonably safe condition and must take all reasonable steps to avoid injury to an invitee.

In some states the distinction among the duties owed to trespassers, licensees, and invitees has been abolished, and all landowners owe the ordinary duty of reasonable care to those on their premises.

Ordinarily, a landlord owes no duty with respect to premises that the landlord has leased to someone else. There are, however, a number of important exceptions.

First, a landlord must exercise reasonable care to inspect and repair parts of the premises that are not exclusively leased to one tenant, such as hallways, stairways, sidewalks, and the like.

Second, a landlord must use ordinary care to see that the premises are safe at the time possession is transferred as regards persons outside the land and in situations where the premises are leased for the purpose of allowing the public to enter, such as the lease of a theater or store.

A landlord is also liable if he or she fails to disclose any unreasonably dangerous condition that exists at the time possession is delivered, if he or she fails to comply with a contractual obligation to make repairs, or if he or she actually makes repairs (whether required to do so or not) but does so negligently.

Until recent years, almost all states followed a contributory negligence rule under which a plaintiff whose own negligence was a contributing cause of his or her injuries was totally barred from all recovery. This harsh rule sometimes had the effect of barring a plaintiff whose negligence was slight when compared to the negligence of the defendant, and the rule has gradually been abandoned. The usual rule is now one of **comparative negligence**: the plaintiff is permitted to recover so long as the plaintiff's negligence is not greater than that of the defendant. The judge or jury is asked to apportion the total negligence between the parties in percentage terms, and the plaintiff's damages are reduced accordingly. Thus, if the plaintiff's fault is determined to represent 30% of the total fault that caused the injury, his or her damages will be reduced by 30%, and the defendant will be liable only for the remaining 70%. This system insures that a plaintiff is penalized for his or her own negligence, yet it prevents the defendant from escaping without liability due to slight negligence by the plaintiff.

Up to this point our discussion has focused on torts in which the tortfeasor possesses some degree of fault. Are there situations in which someone may be held liable in tort despite having acted with the utmost of care? The answer is that there are **strict-liability torts**, the three leading examples of which will be discussed in the following paragraphs.

While most activities result in liability only if the actor is negligent, certain "ultrahazardous" activities may be undertaken only at the actor's own risk. These activities include such dangerous conduct as blasting, use of poisons, and the flying of especially dangerous aircraft. Among the factors to be considered in determining whether an activity is abnormally dangerous are whether it involves a high likelihood of harm, whether the harm is likely to be great, whether the activity can be made safe through reasonable care, whether it is a matter of common usage, whether it is inappropriate for the place where it is carried on, and whether it is valuable to the community. Thus an activity may be abnormally dangerous under some circumstances but not under others.

The owners of wild animals are generally held to be strictly liable to those who are injured by the animals. The status of domesticated animals, such as pets or barnyard animals, is slightly more complicated. Such an animal is treated as a "wild" animal if its owner has reason to know that it has a vicious disposition, but not otherwise. This has given rise to what is sometimes known as the **"one-bite" rule**; that is, that the owner of a cat or dog is not liable on the first occasion on which the pet bites a person. Such a rule is misleading, since the true test is whether the owner should know of the animal's nature and not whether it has been vicious in the past.

By far the most important of the strict liability torts is the liability that a manufacturer or seller bears for defects in products. This is known as **products liability**, and in recent years it has come to represent a substantial fraction of all tort litigation. While at one time products liability existed only under theories of negligence or breach of warranty and was subject to difficult burdens of proof and broad defenses, most states have made products liability a strict liability tort.

In the *Second Restatement of Torts*, Section 402A discusses liability for physical harm to persons or property caused by any defective product that is unreasonably dangerous at the time it leaves the defendant's hands. This rule applies whether or not the user or consumer who is injured dealt directly with the defendant. Thus, a manufacturer is liable even if its product was sold and resold several times before reaching the consumer.

The products liability rule, as adopted by the courts, has two important aspects: (a) the product in question must be defective, and (b) it must be unreasonably dangerous. Both of these elements are required before liability exists.

A "defective" product is one that does not meet the reasonable expectations of the ordinary consumer as to its safety.[9] The defect may be inherent in the product, that is, the product may be improperly designed. Or, it may be properly designed but improperly manufactured, packaged, or labelled. Alternatively, the defect may consist of a failure to provide an adequate warning as to the limitations or dangers of the product or to provide proper instructions for its safe use.

It is immaterial whether the manufacturer or seller knew of the defect, or even whether it was negligent in not knowing of the defect. As with other strict liability torts, liability is imposed without regard to fault. While the defect must be one that existed at the time the product left the defendant's hands, the failure to provide a safeguard against future defects that the defendant knows are likely to occur may itself be a defect.

The second aspect of products liability is that the defect must cause the product to be unreasonably dangerous. It is not enough to show that a product could have been made without the defect: the plaintiff must show that it was unreasonable not to do so. Thus, while products liability is technically a strict liability tort, one of the elements of negligence -- reasonableness -- comes in "through the back door," so to speak, through the requirement of unreasonable danger. In making the determination of reasonableness, the judge or jury must weigh the utility of the product against the risk involved in its use.[10]

In relation to a specific danger created by a product, this means that the feasibility and cost of eliminating the danger must be compared with the danger itself and the risk of injury that it presents. Thus some products, such as certain prescription drugs, may be "unavoidably unsafe," that is, the products may be so useful that they should be marketed despite the fact that there is no way to make them completely safe. In such a case, the manufacturer or seller will not be held liable. The manufacturer or seller may, however, be required to include a warning of the danger if a warning will help to minimize the risk.

A manufacturer or seller is ordinarily not liable if its product is put to an improper use in a manner not contemplated when the product was designed. This defense is, however, subject to an important qualification: the misuse must be of a kind that the defendant could not reasonably expect. Thus, while automobiles need not be built to withstand any type of crash whatsoever, it is to be expected that automobiles will be involved in accidents, and hence the manufacturer must make them as "crashworthy" as is reasonably possible. Misuse may also be unavailable as a defense if an adequate warning might have prevented the misuse.

While contributory and comparative negligence have no place in products liability cases, a few states have an unusual doctrine known as **comparative causation.** Under this doctrine, a manufacturer's liability may be reduced by a percentage that represents the degree to which the plaintiff's misconduct participated in causing the injury, much like a negligent tortfeasor's liability is reduced under comparative negligence.[11]

Two very different types of torts fall under the general heading of nuisance. A **private nuisance** is an interference with a landowner's right to possession and enjoyment of his or her land, while a **public nuisance** is an interference with the rights of the public generally. Nuisance is not, strictly speaking, a separate tort; it is instead a label applied to a variety of torts. Thus there may be negligent nuisances, intentional nuisances, or nuisances for which strict liability is imposed. Public nuisances include such things as "houses of prostitution, gambling dens, hog pens, illegal liquor establishments, indecent exhibitions, bullfights, unauthorized prize fights and the illegal practice of law and medicine."[12]

To be permitted to sue to stop such things, the plaintiff cannot sue simply as a member of the general public but must instead have suffered a specific injury. A private nuisance, on the other hand, involves conduct that interferes with a specific individual's right to enjoyment of a specific piece of land by interfering with access to the land or with its habitability, by reducing its value, or by otherwise unreasonably depriving its owner of its full use. A nuisance may be one that is a nuisance under all circumstances (a **nuisance per se**) or one that is a nuisance only by virtue of the particular circumstances in which it is conducted (a **nuisance per accidents**). As the United States Supreme Court has stated, "A nuisance may be merely a right thing in the wrong place, like a pig in the parlor instead of the barnyard."[13]

There are a variety of torts that do not involve actual personal injury or property damage. Chief among these is the tort of **deceit**, or **fraud**, which consists of the making of a knowingly false representation upon which someone reasonably relies to his or her detriment in deciding to enter into a transaction. Other so-called "**business torts**" include **negligent misrepre-**

sentation, **interference with business relations**, and **unfair competition**. A number of business torts, such as securities fraud, antitrust torts, and the use of deceptive trade practices, are created by statute.

Another group of torts involves interference with personal rights: examples of such torts include **defamation (libel** and **slander)**, **invasion of privacy**, and **malicious prosecution** (sometimes called abuse of process where a civil case is involved).

Other torts involve a combination of personal and financial rights, such as the torts created by Title VII of the Civil Rights Act of 1964 and the Age Discrimination in Employment Act for employment discrimination on grounds of race, sex, religion, national origin, or age.

There are two principal types of damages awarded in tort lawsuits: **compensatory** (or actual) damages; and **punitive** (or **exemplary**) damages. The purpose of compensatory damages is to restore the tort victim to the place the victim would have occupied had the tort not occurred, to the extent that this may be done by a monetary payment. In some cases, a tort may technically have been committed but the victim may have suffered no loss; in such cases, an award of **nominal damages**, usually $1.00, is made.

Punitive damages, on the other hand, are designed to punish the tortfeasor and are awarded only in the case of intentional torts or cases involving so-called "gross" negligence or "willful and wanton misconduct." Some statutory torts have their own damage scheme: for example, damages for antitrust violations are trebled as a way of punishing the wrongdoer. Some statutes also require that a losing defendant pay the plaintiff's attorneys' fees.

Finally, in appropriate cases an **injunction** may be granted to bring a halt to a continuing tort, such as a nuisance or ongoing pattern of harassment.

It is impossible to discuss all of tort law in a few short pages. Entire volumes are written on the subject and, indeed, entire volumes have been written on each of the many topics that have been discussed. The discussion presented in this section is designed to provide a background understanding of the most important aspects of tort law. Many topics have been omitted, while others have been explained in general but not in detail. For a more detailed understanding of particular topics, consult the *Second Restatement of Torts*, published by the American Law Institute, or a good treatise on the subject, such as W. Prosser, *The Law of Torts*.

Contracts.

The second of the three principal branches of the common law is the law of contracts. Like modern tort law, much of modern contract law is derived from an old English writ -- this time the **writ of assumpsit**. The principal difference between contract and tort liability is that, with limited exceptions to be discussed below, no contractual liability can be created except by means of an agreement.

Thus, contractual liability is as infinitely varied as the types of agreements into which individuals may enter. All that is required is that there be an offer and an acceptance, that the contract be of a type which the law will recognize and enforce, and that it be breached by one party with resulting damage to the other. In the pages which follow, we will explore each of these elements. In addition, we will examine the **Uniform**

Commercial Code, a statutory codification of many aspects of the common law of contracts that has been enacted in every state.

Contracts may be broadly grouped into three categories. First are **express contracts,** where the parties have expressly agreed, orally or in writing, that each is to be bound to do certain things. Common examples include real estate leases, bills of sale, and formal employment contracts.

Secondly, a contract may be **implied in fact**. In this type of contract the parties have not formally agreed to be bound, but a mutual intention to make a contract can be inferred from their conduct. For example, a patient who visits a doctor's office usually does not agree with the doctor in advance that he or she will pay a specific fee in exchange for certain specific acts by the doctor. Rather, there is an implied contract by which the doctor agrees to use his or her best efforts to cure the patient, while the patient agrees to pay the doctor's usual and reasonable fee for that service.

It is not necessary that an entire contract be implied: where the parties have made an express contract but have omitted one or more terms, it is possible that their intentions with respect to those terms may be inferred from their conduct. Thus, if a customer has bought widgets from the Acme Widget Company for twenty years, and on each occasion the widgets have been shipped by rail, a "shipment by rail" term may be implied in a sales contract that does not discuss the topic of shipment.[14]

Finally, a contract may be **implied in law**. Such contracts differ from implied in fact contracts in that the parties never reached any kind of agreement, express or implied. This makes the expression "implied in law contract" somewhat misleading, since there is really no contract; indeed, this type of liability is sometimes called **quasi-contractual liability**. In an implied-in-law contract, the law imposes requirements on the parties even though they have not agreed to be bound by those requirements, usually because it would be unfair (or, in legal parlance, would produce **unjust enrichment**) to allow one party to receive a benefit conferred upon him or her by the other without paying for that benefit. For example, in an old Arkansas case a man suffered injuries in a street car wreck and was come upon by a doctor, who treated him in an unsuccessful attempt to save his life. Despite the fact that the victim had been unconscious and so could not possibly have agreed, expressly or by implication from his conduct, to pay for the doctor's services, the court permitted the doctor to recover the reasonable value of his services from the victim's estate.[15]

In order for a binding contract to be formed, there must be an **offer** and an **acceptance**. An offer is no more than a communication by one party to the other that reasonably leads the receiving party to believe that the offering party is willing to enter into a contract. The intention must be to enter into an immediate contract, not merely to set forth the terms under which further negotiations can occur. Thus a statement such as "I will sell you this for $50" is an offer, while a statement such as "My usual price for this is $50" would not be construed as an offer. All the surrounding circumstances, including the language used, the method of communication, the specificity of the terms, and the custom between the parties and in the industry, must be examined to determine if an offer has been made.

An offer remains open until it expires, is withdrawn, is rejected, or is accepted. Some offers, especially those in writing, contain an express expiration date, as "This offer will expire at noon on January 15, 1998, unless accepted before that time." Whether or not an offer contains such a term, the offering party may ordinarily withdraw the offer at any time by communicating that fact to the receiving party.

Exceptions exist where the offering party has been paid something in exchange for making the offer. If the offer states, "For a fee of $1,000, I hereby offer to sell you 1,000 widgets for $10 each at any time during the next six months," such an offer is irrevocable. When a merchant makes a "firm" offer, the merchant promises to keep the offer open for a reasonable time.[16]

An offer also terminates when it is rejected by the receiving party. A rejection may be express, as the statement "I reject your offer." The rejection may occur by lapse of a reasonable time. In addition, any counteroffer that varies the terms of the original offer is a rejection. The exchanges "I will buy that for $50," followed by "I will sell it for $100," show that the original $50 offer from the buyer is rejected and replaced by a new $100 offer from the seller.

Once an offer is terminated by expiration, withdrawal, or rejection, it cannot be accepted to form a binding contract. If not terminated, however, an offer may be accepted in any reasonable manner. Acceptance creates a binding contract and terminates the right to withdraw the offer.

Offers may be divided into two broad categories: those which contemplate a promise in exchange for a promise, called offers for **bilateral contracts** ("I promise to pay you $1,000 if you will promise to deliver 1,000 widgets") and those which contemplate actual performance as an acceptance, offers for **unilateral contracts** ("I promise to pay you $1,000 if you will deliver 1,000 widgets").

Where an offer makes plain that only acceptance by performance is contemplated, an acceptance by promise is insufficient; on the other hand, acceptance of an offer for a bilateral contract may be by promise or by performance. Most offers do not make plain which type of acceptance they seek; in such circumstances Section 2-206 of the Uniform Commercial Code permits any reasonable form of acceptance. The ordinary rule is that an acceptance may not vary any of the terms of the offer: that is, an offer is a "take it or leave it" proposition.

Section 2-207 of the Uniform Commercial Code creates an exception to this rule, designed to cover the so-called "battle-of-the-forms" situation where the offer and the acceptance contain differing "boilerplate" language, as often happens in dealings between large companies. In such a situation, additional terms in the acceptance become part of the contract unless objected to by the offering party, and those terms plus the terms on which the parties can agree become the contract.

In order for a contract to be binding, it must be sufficiently specific. Thus it must identify the parties and the subject matter; a contract to sell "a piece of land" or "some corn" is not specific enough to be enforced. It is not necessary that all items be spelled out: in the absence of terms dealing with these subjects, the law will imply a reasonable price, a delivery of goods in one lot, a place for delivery, shipment within a reasonable time, payment within a reasonable time, a requirement that a choice of options under the contract be made in good faith, and sometimes even a reasonable quantity.

If the contract deals with these subjects, however, it must be sufficiently specific to identify the intentions of the parties. A contract to sell goods at a price of "$10 to $20 each" is too vague, since the parties have given some indication of their intent but have not given enough information to allow a court to determine what they meant. Similarly, an agreement to sell "at a price to be negotiated later" is not binding unless and until a price is agreed upon.

A contract may not ordinarily be enforced unless the party seeking enforcement has given some legal consideration in exchange for the promise or performance of the other party. **Consideration** consists of an act that a party performs or promises to perform, even though he or she has no legal duty to do so, or **forbearance** or a promise of forbearance from an act that he or she has a legal right to do.

A famous example is the case in which an uncle promised his nephew $5,000 if the nephew would refrain from drinking, smoking, swearing, and gambling until he reached 21. Consideration was held to be present even though the forbearance by the nephew had benefitted his health and morals, since he had refrained from doing things which he had a legal right to do.[17] Note, however, that had the promise been only to refrain from smoking marijuana, there would have been no consideration, since in that case the nephew would not be refraining from doing that which he had a legal right to do. Similarly, a promise to do something, such as pay a debt, that the party is already under a legal obligation to do will not, absent a bona fide dispute about the existence of the legal obligation, serve as sufficient consideration.

Consideration must be bargained for; thus a promise to a derelict that "I will give you a new coat if you will come to my store and pick it up" is not binding, even though the derelict does something he or she had a legal right not to do.

Under limited circumstances, a contract will be enforced despite a lack of consideration. In some states a contract that contains the seal of a party (either a genuine embossed, printed, or attached seal or the word "SEAL") will be enforced against a party despite the absence of consideration by the other party. The Uniform Commercial Code abolishes this effect of the seal with respect to sales of goods.

More importantly, under the doctrine of **promissory estoppel** or **detrimental reliance**, a promise that the promising party should reasonably expect to cause definite and substantial reliance by the other party, and that does cause such reliance, is binding even if the other party furnishes no consideration. A classic example is a case where a person promises to make a contribution to a charitable organization, and the organization builds a building or otherwise commits itself in reliance on the promise. Even though there is no consideration on the part of the charity, such a promise will be enforced.

Once a contract is created, it must be interpreted, that is, the words and phrases in the contract must be examined to determine what the parties intended. Under the **parol evidence rule**, statements -- usually oral -- outside a written contract may not be used to contradict the terms of the contract. Thus, if a written contract specifies a price of $10 per widget, the buyer will not be permitted to testify that the buyer and the salesperson had agreed to a 10% discount for a net price of $9 per widget.

In short, written terms control over oral agreements to the contrary. Typewritten terms control over printed terms to the contrary, and handwritten terms control over both printed and typewritten terms.

Where the oral terms do not contradict the written contract but instead supplement it, the parol evidence rule is more complicated. Where the parties intend that the written contract is to be a full and complete expression of their agreement, no additional terms are admissible. In other circumstances, however, additional terms are admissible so long as they are consistent with the written terms.[18]

There is a variety of reasons why a contract or an individual term in a contract may be held to be unenforceable. First among these is the **Statute of Frauds**, a 1677 English statute that has been adopted in each of the United States, requiring certain types of contracts to be in writing. While there are many categories of contracts that are subject to this requirement, the most important contracts subject to the Statute of Frauds are:

- contracts for the sale of an interest in land
- contracts which cannot be performed within one year
- contracts for the sale of goods worth $500 or more.

The last category is governed by §2-201 of the Uniform Commercial Code. Note that for the second category the Statute does not come into play whenever a contract may take more than one year to perform, but only when it must take that long. For example, a lease for two years is covered by the Statute of Frauds, but a lease for two years or until the tenant dies, whichever is earlier, is not, since the latter contract may or may not last more than one year.

A formal written contract signed by both parties is not necessary under the Statute, but there must be at least a memorandum of the transaction signed by the party against whom the contract is to be enforced.

Some contracts are unenforceable because they are illegal. This may mean that the making of the contract is itself a crime, as in the case of contracts for criminal acts, gambling contracts, or antitrust price-fixing agreements. The most famous case along these lines is *Everet v. Williams*, decided by the English Court of Exchequer in 1725. In that case, one highwayman sued another for breach of a partnership agreement to divide the profits of their endeavors. Not only did the court dismiss the case, but it fined the plaintiffs' lawyers, and both plaintiff and defendant were later caught and hanged!

A contract may be unenforceable for "illegality" even if its making was not a crime. Examples of this type of contract are contracts involving usurious interest rates or leases of property that violate health or building codes.

Some contracts do not involve any direct illegality but are nevertheless unenforceable because the bargain is so one-sided that enforcement would be unjust. As the United States Supreme Court stated in *Scott v. United States*,[19] "[i]f a contract be unreasonable and unconscionable, but not void for fraud, a court of law will give to the party who sues for its breach damages, not according to its letter, but only such as he is equitably entitled to."[20]

Only where there is a gross imbalance of bargaining power resulting in extremely unfavorable terms to the weaker party will a contract be voided as unconscionable. Such cases usually involve a contract of **adhesion**, that is, a standardized contract, usually preprinted, to which the weaker party -- often the buyer -- must agree if the weaker party wishes to do business with the stronger party.

A contract entered into by a minor, an insane person, or one so intoxicated that he or she does not understand what he or she is doing, is ordinarily not enforceable against that person. An exception is created for contracts involving necessities: while no express or implied contract is created due to the contracting party's incapacity, the law implies a quasi-contract to pay the reasonable value of the necessary goods or services. Note that the contract may be unenforceable against the person without capacity, but it is not unenforceable against the other party. Minors, for example, can enforce their contracts like anyone else.

A contract entered into by one who does not have capacity to contract may be ratified once the incapacity is removed. Thus, if an adult ratifies a contract made by him or her while a minor, it becomes fully enforceable.

Contracts may also be avoided for fraud, misrepresentation, **duress**, or **undue influence**. Fraud consists of the making of a knowingly false representation, which representation is reasonably relied upon by the other contracting party in entering into a contract he or she would not otherwise have made. There are two types of fraud: **intrinsic fraud** (sometimes called **fraud in the factum**) and **extrinsic fraud** (sometimes called **fraud in the inducement**).

Intrinsic fraud occurs when the party is not aware of the nature of the agreement into which he or she is entering, as where a person signs a release, having been told that it is not a release but something else. Extrinsic fraud occurs when the party is aware of the bargain he or she is making but has been induced to make the agreement by a deliberate false representation.

Duress and undue influence, on the other hand, consist of pressure that is so severe that the contracting party's will and freedom of choice are overcome. For example, a contract signed at gunpoint would be voidable for duress. Duress need not be physical and may consist of an economic threat that, under the circumstances, operates to deprive someone of free choice.[21] Undue influence consists of similar pressure of a moral rather than a physical or economic kind.[22]

There are a variety of ways in which a contractual duty may be discharged. The most obvious of these is by performance of the duty. A duty is also discharged where it becomes illegal or impossible to perform, as, for example, where a concert pianist contracts to give a recital but is taken ill and cannot do so.

Sometimes a duty is discharged by the fact that an event upon which the duty is conditioned never comes to pass, as where a house is insured against fire but no fire occurs.

A duty may be modified or discharged by contract in a variety of ways:

- the contract giving rise to the duty may be modified or cancelled by agreement of the parties

- a dispute over the rights and obligations of the parties may be compromised (called an **accord and satisfaction**)

- the parties may agree with a third party that the third party will take over some or all of the contractual obligations (called a **novation**).

A contract may also be **rescinded** by a court due to illegality, incapacity, fraud, or other reasons.

Contractual damages are substantially different from tort damages. While tort damages are based on the notion of restitution, that is, that a party should be put in the position he or she would have occupied if the tort had not occurred, contract damages do not seek to put the injured party in the place he or she would have occupied had no contract been made. Instead, contractual recovery is based on an **expectation theory**: that is, that the injured party should be placed in the position he or she would have occupied if the contract had been fully performed.

Thus, one who pays $50 in exchange for an item worth $75 but does not receive the item is entitled not only to restitution of the $50 paid, but also to recovery of the $25 profit that would have made had there been no breach.

As with tort damages, injunctive relief is sometimes called for: where damages are inadequate to restore a party to the party's rightful place, as in contracts for the sale of land or unique goods, **specific performance** may be ordered. The breaching party is in effect forced by court order to comply with the terms of the contract. Where a contract is avoided due to fraud, incapacity, or the like, the court may order rescission of the contract, whereby each party returns to the other that which the party has received and the contract is treated as void.

The Uniform Commercial Code deals with most of the topics discussed above in connection with sales of goods. An important aspect of the UCC is its treatment of warranties. Under the UCC there are five basic types of warranties:

- express warranties, consisting of representations of fact, promises, and descriptions made by the seller, as a limited warranty on a household product

- general implied warranties
- three specific implied warranties that arise by operation of law:
    - implied warranty of title, that the goods belong to the seller
    - implied warranty of merchantability, that the goods are of average quality, fit for ordinary purposes, and are adequately contained, packaged, and labeled
    - implied warranty of fitness for a particular purpose, that the goods are fit for any particular purposes for which the buyer is acquiring them and of which the seller is aware.

The UCC contains provisions governing the extent and manner in which these warranties may be disclaimed.

An important variety of specialized contract, governed by a Article Three of the UCC, is that known as **commercial paper**. Commercial paper exists in two forms:

- **promissory notes**, which are written contracts to pay a sum of money to a specified individual or to a person designated by the individual ("to the order")
- drafts, which are written orders to a third party directing the third party to pay a sum of money to the order of a specified person.

Checks are an important form of draft; a check is merely a draft that is drawn on a bank and payable on demand. The most important feature of notes and drafts is that they are **negotiable**. This means that a person to whom they are transferred ordinarily is not subject to any defenses (such as fraud, lack of consideration, or other contractual defenses that have been previously discussed) of which the transferee was unaware when he or she acquired the notes or drafts. This important aspect of commercial paper renders it especially useful in a commercial setting: checks, certificates of deposit, and most corporate and governmental bonds flow freely back and forth from owner to owner with little risk on the part of the purchaser that he or she will be subject to defenses of which he or she is unaware.

A note or draft (sometimes referred to as a **negotiable instrument**) may be negotiated from one owner to another by **indorsement**, which consists of the signature of the holder, sometimes with language such as "Pay to the order of John Smith." An indorsement makes the indorser liable to pay the instrument if the maker or the party against whom it is drawn does not. In this manner a "bounced" check is returned from one indorser to another farther up the chain, until finally the check comes to rest in the hands of the party to whom the check is made payable. This party must bear the loss unless he or she can obtain payment from the signer.

Article Nine of the Uniform Commercial Code deals with **secured transactions**. This branch of the law is a marriage between contract law and property law. A secured transaction is one in which a party obtains or retains a **security interest** in goods or other personal property. A security interest is a **lien or mortgage**, as a mortgage on real property, which gives the owner a right to sell or take possession of the property in the event that the secured debt is not paid.

In order to be valid, a security interest must ordinarily be recorded in the office of the Secretary of State or County Clerk, just as a real estate mortgage must ordinarily be recorded. The Uniform Commercial Code sets up an elaborate system of priorities among the owner of the property, the various parties holding security interests, and unsecured creditors. If the debtor goes into bankruptcy, these priorities are further affected by the Federal Bankruptcy Code.

In recent years, statutes other than the Uniform Commercial Code have come to play an important role in contract law. These include the

- Uniform Consumer Credit Code
- Consumer Credit Protection Act, which includes the Truth-in-Lending Act
- Fair Credit Reporting Act
- Equal Credit Opportunity Act
- Uniform Fraudulent Conveyance Act
- Magnuson-Moss Warranty Act
- Federal Bankruptcy Code

Various states have their own consumer protection statutes. Also important are various regulations adopted pursuant to these statutes, including the Truth-in-Lending regulations adopted by the Federal Reserve Board and various regulations adopted by the Federal Trade Commission under the Federal Trade Commission Act.

For more detailed information on contract law, you should consult the Uniform Commercial Code, the American Law Institute's *Restatement (Second) of Contracts*, or any good treatise on the law of contracts, such as those by Williston or

Corbin on general contract law or by White and Summers on the Uniform Commercial Code.

Real Property.

The law of real property is by far the most ancient of our inheritances from the common law of England, where it began to develop shortly after the Norman Conquest in 1066. The common law of real property owes its origin to the feudal system in operation in medieval England. Under this system, the ultimate title to all lands in England, and some other places as well, was vested in the king. The king would make grants of land to nobles of various ranks in exchange for their agreements of support, both financial and military. These nobles, called tenants-in-chief, in turn made grants to squires, knights, and other intermediate-level landholders called mesne lords, again in exchange for their support. Those to whom grants were made in turn made grants of their own, and so on down to the level of the lowest peasants.

Each landholder or tenant swore an oath of homage to the landlord and agreed to perform certain services in exchange for the right to hold the land. The landlords, on the other hand, possessed certain rights, such as the right to a payment by a tenant's heir upon the tenant's death (called "relief") and the right to choose whom the tenant would marry. Most early real property law developed as a means of thwarting various legal devices by which the landlords would otherwise have been deprived of their feudal rights.

Under modern property law, as under the feudal system, the owner of land may grant to another some or all of the rights in the land which the owner possesses. The various types of ownership interests which may be created are known as **estates**

in land. These interests may be as varied as the imagination of the granting party, the **grantor**, permits. Thus, estates in land may be conveyed that entitle the receiving party, or **grantee**, to possession and use of the land in perpetuity, or for the next 1/10 of a second, or until such time, if any, as Liechtenstein invades Monaco.

Nevertheless, there are certain types of estates in land that represent the bundles of ownership rights that are most commonly conveyed. The most common estate in land is known as the **fee simple**, representing complete ownership of the land. The grant of a fee simple is commonly made by deeding the property "to A and his or her heirs," but any words which indicate an intent to give A the total ownership rights in the property will suffice. A fee simple estate may be subject to certain conditions, as

- "to A and her heirs, but if the premises shall ever be used for gambling then the grantor may reenter and repossess the premises." This is known as a **fee simple subject to a condition subsequent** and may expire on the happening of a specified event.

- "to A and his heirs so long as the land is used for residential purposes." This is a **fee simple determinable**.

Or, the grant may be a **fee simple absolute**, where the grantee has the maximum possible ownership rights subject to no conditions whatsoever.

An estate in land of great importance in early England but of only marginal relevance today is the **fee tail**, by which land was granted to an individual and passed to his lineal descendants until such time, if any, as the line of descendants ran out.

An estate in land whereby the land is granted to an individual for the duration of his or her lifetime is known, not surprisingly, as a **life estate**. A life estate, ordinarily created by using words such as "to A for life," may be created in one person with reference to the life of another ("to A for the life of B"). This is known by the old French name of an **estate pur autre vie** ("for the life of another").

The fee simple, fee tail, and life estate are known as **freehold estates**, and it is these estates to which we normally refer when we state that an individual "owns" a piece of land. There are, however, several other types of estates in land, as anyone who has ever rented an apartment knows well. These are known as **leasehold estates**.

The most important leasehold estate is the **term of years**. A term of years gives the grantee the right to the possession and use of the property for a specified period of time, which, despite the name of the estate, need not be for one year or more. Thus, any fixed-term lease, whether it is for six months or ninety-nine years, creates a term of years.

The other common leasehold estate is the **periodic tenancy**. This estate is a leasehold estate for a given period of time that automatically renews itself unless one party notifies the other that renewal is not desired. A periodic tenancy may be from day to day, week to week, month to month, year to year, or may have any other fixed renewal period. Many leases for a fixed period, which thus create a term of years, contain provisions for continuation beyond the expiration date of the lease on a year-to-year or month-to-month basis, thereby creating a periodic tenancy following the initial term of years. The notice required to terminate a year-to-year tenancy must be given six months in advance of the termination date, while other periodic tenancies may be terminated on notice equal to the period of the tenancy. The notice must terminate the tenancy at the end of a period and not in the middle of the period.

The final leasehold estate is the **tenancy at will**. This estate in land is terminable without advance notice by either party and is thus the most fragile estate in land which can be imagined. True tenancies at will are rare, for the usual effect of periodic payment of rent for a tenancy at will is to convert the tenancy into a periodic tenancy. A tenancy at will terminates automatically if either party dies or if the landlord sells the property.

In addition to the freehold and leasehold estates described above, there are a variety of interests in land that do not rise to the level of estates. There are four main categories of such interests, the most important of which is the **easement**. An easement is a right to make some specified use of the land of another. The most common easements are the **utility easement**, where the utility company is granted the right to erect poles or bury underground cables or pipes, and the **right-of-way easement**, where a landowner is granted the right to pass over land of his or her neighbor in order to reach the landowner's own property.

Some easements, especially right-of-way easements, may be created by implication; thus where a grantor conveys an inaccessible portion of his or her land, the grantee receives not only that land but an implied easement, known as an **easement appurtenant**, entitling the grantee to travel over the rest of the grantor's land to reach the conveyed property.

Other non-estate interests in land include:

- profits (sometimes called **profits a prendre**), which are rights to sever minerals or crops from the land

- **licenses**, which create a limited right to use the land for a specific purpose, as a theater ticket

- **restrictive covenants**, which are placed in a deed to limit the uses to which the land may be put or the individuals to whom it may be conveyed.

These limited interests may assume major importance in a particular transaction or type of transaction. Profits for the extraction of minerals -- commonly called mineral leases, although that term is misleading -- are the means by which most mineral exploration takes place. Restrictive covenants prohibiting sale to ethnic groups constituted a major source of housing discrimination until they were struck down by the United States Supreme Court in *Shelley v. Kraemer.*

There are a variety of ways in which two or more persons may concurrently own a single piece of land. First among these is the **tenancy in common**, in which the owners hold undivided interests in the land. By this is meant that each has the right to full and complete possession and use of all the land, subject only to the same right as to all the other tenants in common. If land held by tenancy in common is leased or put to productive use, the tenants in common all share in the profits. Note that it is not necessary that each tenant in common be entitled to the same undivided interest in the land; a tenancy in common may be created where A owns 2/3 and B owns 1/3. Any tenant in common may demand a partition of the land, that is, may demand that he or she receive exclusive title to a portion of the land representing his or her fair share. If the parties are unable to agree on a satisfactory partition, a lawsuit seeking a partition may be brought and the court will divide the land equitably.

An important form of concurrent ownership, similar in most respects to the tenancy in common, is the **joint tenancy**. The owners of a joint tenancy bear the same relationship to one another as in the case of a tenancy in common, with one important exception: each joint tenant has a **right of survivorship**. This means that upon the death of one joint tenant, that tenant's interest automatically passes by operation of law to the other joint tenant or tenants. As tenants in common, joint tenants may demand a partition or may convey their interests to a third party. Such an act, however, operates to destroy the right of survivorship, leaving the new owner in possession of only a tenancy in common and eliminating the right of the owner who has demanded partition to any of his or her former co-tenant's interests on such co-tenant's death.

A specialized form of the joint tenancy that is important in most states is the **tenancy by the entireties** between a husband and wife. In states that follow the common-law system of marital property, a conveyance to a husband and wife as joint tenants creates a special type of joint tenancy, in which the parties may not convey their separate interests or demand a partition, and in which the husband is entitled to sole possession and control of the property and the rents and profits from it.

This inequitable arrangement does not exist in states that follow the community property system. Instead, all property acquired with community funds is community property belonging to both husband and wife, Whether the grant is made to the husband or the wife or both is not controlling. It is not possible to create a joint tenancy between a husband and wife where the property is community property.

The tenancy in common, joint tenancy, and tenancy by the entireties are, of course, not the only means by which more than one person may hold an interest in the same piece of land. Any conveyance of an estate less than a fee simple absolute necessarily involves a second owner who owns the remaining property interest (called a **reversion** if owned by the grantor and a **remainder** if owned by a third party). Thus where a grantor who owns a fee simple conveys "to A for life," the owners of the property are A and the grantor: A is entitled to use and possession for A's lifetime, and the grantor regains the property thereafter.

An important form of co-ownership is created through **mortgages** (sometimes termed **deeds of trust**) and other forms of **liens**. A mortgage is an interest in land whereby the owner of the interest (the **mortgagee**) may seize and sell the land (**foreclosure**) if a debt owed to the owner by the holder of the property (the **mortgagor**) is not paid when due. Virtually every modern real estate sale involves at least one mortgage, and a transaction involving the construction of a large office building may involve several mortgages, including one to secure payment of the price of the land, another for interim construction costs, and a third for permanent financing. In some states a mortgage transaction is accomplished by conveying the property to a **trustee**, usually a representative of the mortgagee, who is to hold the property on behalf of the mortgagee, to allow the mortgagor to use the land, and to release the trust if the mortgage indebtedness is fully paid.

A mortgage is one form of **lien**, or security interest, in land, arising from the consent of the owner. Other forms of lien arise by operation of law, irrespective of the owner's consent. Among these is the **vendor's lien**, which is a lien in favor of the seller of property to insure that the seller receives the full purchase price. Where construction work is performed on property, **mechanic's liens** in favor of contractors or workmen and **materialmen's liens** in favor of suppliers of construction materials may arise to secure the payment of those individuals' charges. **Tax liens** may arise to secure payment of unpaid taxes, while a **judgment lien** is conferred upon the winner of a lawsuit against the lands of the loser to secure payment of the judgment. There is also a group of miscellaneous liens, such as hospital liens, to secure other types of payments.

A conveyance of land is generally accomplished by means of a **deed**, which is a written record of the fact that land has been transferred from one party to another. (In medieval England, transfer was accomplished by the parties' going to the land and the grantor's giving the grantee a clod of earth or twig to symbolize transfer of the land; this ceremony, known as **livery of seisin**, has long ago given way to more formal methods of transfer.) In the typical real estate transaction, delivery of a deed is usually preceded by the signing of a contract of sale that sets out the terms of the agreement, including the price to be paid, the method of financing, and the date and procedures for the **closing**, where the deeds, mortgages, and money are transferred. Under the Statute of Frauds, discussed briefly above with reference to contract law, all contracts for the transfer of an estate in land (except for leases of property for one year or less) must be in writing.

There are three types of deeds in common use today. The first is the **general warranty deed**, which includes a warranty (promise) that the grantor holds good title to the land (that is, that he or she owns an estate at least as big as the one he or she is conveying). A **special warranty deed** promises only that the grantor is giving the grantee as good a title as the grantor originally received from his or her grantor, or, in other words, that the grantor has done nothing to impair the title to the property during the grantor's ownership of it. Finally, a **quitclaim deed** contains no warranties, giving the grantee whatever interest in the property (if any) that his or her grantor had at the time of the deed. A contract of sale will typically state the type of deed to be delivered, and ordinarily requires that the grantor have "good and marketable title," that is, a title free of liens and other actual or potential ownership interests in third parties (these are known as **clouds on the title**).

Since there is ordinarily no reliable way to ascertain the identity of the owner from the appearance of the land itself, a system of deed recording has been developed to make this information readily available. Under this system, every deed and deed of trust, together with records of certain other interests such as some liens, is recorded in the County Clerk's office in the county in which the land is located. (Leases may be, but are not often, recorded.) Each document is indexed under the name of the grantor and under the name of the grantee. By means of these indices, the chain of grantors and grantees of a particular piece of land may be traced: this is known as a **title search**. Beginning with the most recent owner, the searcher goes back through the grantee index until he or she finds the deed by which that person received the property, doing the same for each previous owner until the researcher has traced the title as far back as he or she wishes to go. The researcher can then go forward through the grantor index to be sure that no previous owner tried to sell the property to two different purchasers, or created any other cloud on the title. The researcher may prepare an **abstract of title**, which is a summary of the transactions by which title to the property has changed hands over the years, and a **title opinion** that the seller holds good title. This will give the current purchaser a guarantee that the seller holds the property in an unbroken chain of title. The purchaser may also obtain a policy of **title insurance** from an insurance company that will make good any losses if it is later discovered that there is a defect in the title.

In order to make the recording system work, it is necessary that purchasers be protected from the effects of deeds that are not properly recorded. Although this might have been done by making all unrecorded deeds null and void, the same result can be accomplished by less drastic measures. Hence by statute a **bona fide purchaser**, that is, one who is unaware of any ownership interests not reflected in the deed records, takes a title to the property that is free of all unrecorded deeds and other interests. Thus it is extremely dangerous to fail to record a deed, the third party will receive full title and the holder of the unrecorded deed will receive nothing. While this may seem harsh, it is the only means by which someone who has searched the deed records may be sure that he or she is getting full title to the property.

In addition to the so-called "record interests," which one may find recorded in the deed records, there are certain non-recorded interests. Chief among these is **adverse possession**. Under this doctrine, a party who remains in open, continuous, and adverse possession of a tract of land for a specified amount of time (twenty years in most states) acquires title to the land. In order for a claim of adverse possession to be made, the party must possess the land without the permission of the true owner and must claim openly that he or she has a right to be on the land. Adverse possessors may add together the periods of their possession of the land; thus if one adverse possessor remains on the land for ten years and then sells to another, the second party need remain only another ten years to acquire complete title. One of the most frequent applications of adverse possession today is the situation where land has been incorrectly surveyed and a fence or building encroaches on a neighbor's land; unless the neighbor takes legal action within twenty years, the owner of the fence or building acquires by adverse possession the land on which the office or building is located.

Ownership of land, even in the case of a fee simple "absolute," is never absolute. A variety of governmental regulations control the use to which land may be put. Chief among these are **zoning ordinances**, which in most cities regulate the use to which land may be put and the structures which may be erected on it.[23] When property is first brought under a zoning ordinance, structures and uses that are inconsistent with the zoning classification are permitted to remain as **nonconforming uses**, but such uses may not be changed or expanded. Hence the property eventually comes under the zoning law.

Another important governmental interference with the unfettered use and possession of land is the right of **eminent domain**. Where a specific tract of land is needed for a governmental purpose, such as the construction of a road, park, or governmental building, a governmental entity having the right of eminent domain may force the owner to sell it by bringing a **condemnation** proceeding in court. The court will order the land to be transferred and will determine a fair price that the owner must be paid. The Fifth Amendment of the United States Constitution provides that private property shall not "be taken for public use, without just compensation," and the constitutions of many states contain similar prohibitions. Some state constitutions also prohibit the use of the eminent domain power for private uses of the condemned land.

The assessment of real estate taxes and assessments for improvements to streets, sewers, sidewalks, and the like, are yet other examples of limitations on the complete ownership of land.

In addition to the legal ownership of land is its **equitable ownership**. Equitable interests in land are the product of the old English courts of chancery, which developed new remedies and the legal institutions in an attempt to compete with the common law courts. Today, although law courts and equity courts have been merged in the federal system and in almost every state, these equitable interests survive and play an important role in real property law. Two equitable devices are especially important. The first is the doctrine of **equitable conversion**, under which a contract for the sale of land creates not only a legal contractual obligation for the seller to deliver a deed (which in turn delivers the legal title to the land) but an equitable title to the land, which arises on behalf of the buyer as soon as the contract is signed. This permits the buyer to avail himself or herself of the equitable remedy of specific performance (see the section on contract law) to force the seller to go through with the sale. It also means, however, that the buyer becomes responsible for such items as fire insurance (absent a contractual provision to the contrary) and that the seller may force him or her to buy through specific performance.

The **trust** is another institution developed by the equity courts. In a trust transaction, real or personal property is conveyed by one individual (the **settlor** or **trustor**) to another (the **trustee**), who receives the legal title to the property but holds it for the benefit of a third party (the **beneficiary** or **cestui que trust**), who holds the equitable title. While the settlor, trustee, and beneficiary are usually different individuals, it is possible for two of these to be the same person. A trust may be **revocable** or **irrevocable** and may be created by a deed (an **inter vivos trust**) or by will (a **testamentary trust**). A typical trust instrument contains provisions describing the interests of the various beneficiaries, the powers of the trustee, and the way in which the trust will terminate.

An important pitfall for the drafter of a trust or other instrument conveying property is the common-law **rule against perpetuities**. Any thorough discussion of the rule against perpetuities would occupy an entire chapter and would require a background in real property law beyond that of the average legal assistant. Indeed, one court has held the rule to be so complex that an attorney is sometimes not liable for malpractice for drafting an instrument that violates the rule.[24] Suffice it to say that the rule establishes a time limit -- the lifetimes of those who are alive at the time the instrument takes effect, plus twenty-one years -- beyond which no interest may vest under the instrument. Any interest that might theoretically take effect after this time is void, no matter how remote the possibility that this will occur and without regard for whether it does in fact occur. Some states have enacted so-called "wait-and-see" statutes, under which an interest is not void unless it does in fact take effect too late.

Although no discussion of real property law would be complete without some mention of land-tenant law, few generalizations can be made for the simple reason that most obligations of landlord and tenant are created by the lease contract that they make, and hence may vary considerably depending on their agreement. There are, however, a few rules which apply to virtually every lease.

A lease creates rights and obligations in each party. The landlord is obliged to provide possession of the premises, together with **quiet enjoyment** (this does not refer to noise, but to possession without interference). Some leases also impose an obligation to make repairs, to provide hot water or other utilities, or perhaps to provide security services, but the landlord ordinarily has no obligation to provide these items unless the lease so specifies. Where the landlord so interferes with the tenant's right to possession that the interference is equivalent to a forcible eviction, there is a **constructive eviction** and the tenant is relieved of any further obligations. Thus where the landlord is obligated to provide water but ceases to do so, the tenant may vacate the premises and cease paying rent. Of course, the tenant has the right to use all other available legal remedies for breach of contract, which may include money damages or an injunction. When the landlord transfers ownership of the premises, the new owner is subject to all the obligations under the lease which "touch and concern" the land, including obligations to repair, to provide utilities, and the like.

The tenant's primary obligation under a lease is to pay rent, but this is not the tenant's only obligation. The premises must be kept free from waste, that is, significant negligent or intentional destruction or damage. If the tenant alters the premises without the landlord's consent, the tenant must restore them to their previous condition before the end of the tenancy. A tenant is ordinarily under no obligation to make repairs (except for repairs that are necessary to prevent damage to the property, such as replacing broken windows) but may contract in the lease to provide repairs. The tenant may transfer his or her rights and obligations to another tenant unless the lease prohibits this. A transfer of all the tenant's interest is known as an **assignment of the lease**, whereby the new tenant becomes responsible to the landlord for all of the obligations under the lease. A transfer of less than all rights is a **sublease**, under which the tenant becomes a new junior landlord and the new tenant owes his or her obligations to the old tenant, who in turn owes obligations to the landlord. In neither case is the old tenant excused from his or her obligations to the landlord.

A tenant who "holds over" on the premises after a lease has expired may be forced by the landlord into a new periodic tenancy. Thus a tenant who leases from January to December of 1993 but holds over into January of 1994 may be forced by the landlord to pay rent through December of 1994, due to the creation of an implied year-to-year tenancy. At common law a landlord could also use force to evict a tenant in wrongful possession of the premises, but modern statutes prohibit so-called **forcible entry**. On the other hand, the common law gave the landlord no remedy other than a suit for breach of contract where the tenant was not in wrongful possession but had unjustifiably defaulted on his or her obligations. Modern statutes create a new action of **ejectment** (sometimes misleadingly referred to as **forcible entry and detainer**) that permits the landlord to regain the premises and force the tenant to vacate with a minimum of delay and legal red tape.

Important reference works on the law of real property include *A. Casner, American Law of Property* (1952), and the American Institute's Restatement of Property. The original Restatement of Property was published in five volumes from 1938 to 1944. The Restatement of the Law, Second, Property 2nd, has added a volume on Landlord and Tenant and four volumes on donative transfers. The Third Restatement, printed in draft form, contains new information on mortgages and servitudes and additional material on donative transfers.

Wills and Intestate Succession.

Wills were not generally recognized by the common law before the Statute of Wills in 1540. Prior to that time, land, which in early days constituted the bulk of all wealth, passed by operation of law to a feudal tenant's **heirs**, that is, his closest surviving descendants or other relatives. The heirs paid a relief to the landlord. In the event that there were no heirs, the property returned to the lord by **escheat**.

Since the Statute of Wills, property ordinarily descends by will to those designated by the maker of the will, a **testator**. Nevertheless, feudal heirship still survives in the form of modern statutes that define the distribution of the property of a person who dies without a will, termed **intestate succession**, and property continues to escheat to the state in case where no heir can be found.

The statutes that govern the intestate succession of property employ two main systems for distribution. When property passes **per capita**, each person who is entitled to share takes an equal share. Imagine a decedent who leaves three surviving children, two surviving grandchildren, and two surviving great-grand-children in the following manner in the following diagram. If the decedent's property passes per capita, each of the seven surviving descendants will take a 1/7 share.

Property may also pass **per stirpes**, whereby each descendant takes a share that represents a proportionate distribution of the property at each succeeding generation. In the example given, each living child would take 1/4 of any property passing per stirpes, since there were four children altogether. Each surviving grandchild would take 1/3 of his or her parent's 1/4 share (that is, 1/12), since the deceased child had a total of three children. The two great-grandchildren would each take 1/2 of their parent's 1/12 share (that is, 1/24). The total of these shares (1/4 + 1/4 + 1/4 + 1/12 + 1/12 +1/24 + 1/24) adds up, as it must, to 100% of the property.

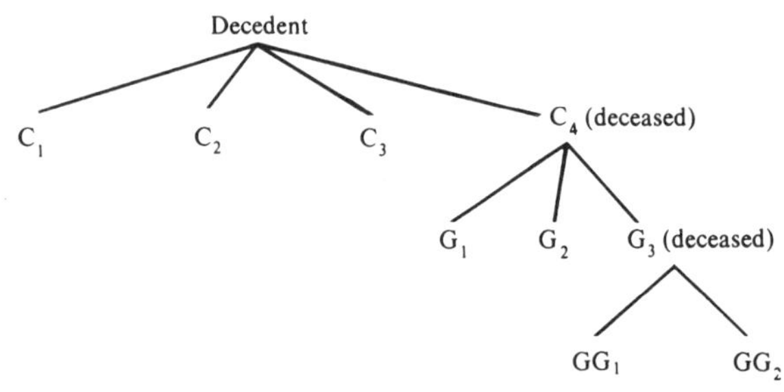

Intestate succession often depends on the type of property involved (real or personal, community or separate), as well as the identity of the survivors. The distribution scheme is summarized in the accompanying table. Note that the spouse always gets at least 1/2 of the community property -- this is his or her community share of that property, of which the spouse cannot be deprived by the death of his or her spouse.

Special rules govern inheritance by adopted children, stepchildren, illegitimate children, and half-brothers and half-sisters. Adopted children may inherit from their natural parents (but not vice versa) and also inherit from their adoptive parents, with respect to whom they are treated as any other children.

A child born out wedlock inherits from his or her mother and inherits from his father if the father has later married the mother or if the father has acknowledged paternity in writing. The Supreme Court held in *Trimble v. Gordon*[25] that certain statutes limiting inheritance by illegitimate children are unconstitutionally discriminatory. Half-brothers and half-sisters inherit half as much as would full-blooded siblings, while stepchildren have no inheritance rights unless adopted.

Example of Intestate Succession

Type of Property	Survived By: Spouse Only	Spouse and Descendants	Descendants Only	Neither Spouse Nor Descendants
Community Property	all to spouse	½ to spouse ½ to descendants (*per stirpes*)	there can be no community property, where the spouse does not survive, since the death of the spouse destroys the community	
Separate Real Property	½ to spouse ½ to parents or collateral relatives	⅓ life estate to spouse ⅓ remainder + ⅔ outright to descendants	all to descendants	½ to each parent *or* ½ to surviving parent and ½ to brothers & sisters or their descendants *or*
Separate Personal Property	all to spouse	⅓ to spouse ⅔ to descendants	all to descendants	all to brothers & sisters or their descendants *or* all to other collateral relatives

The intestate succession laws attempt to make the distribution of property that, it is assumed, most people would want to make. If, however, the scheme set up by those laws is not to an individual's liking, he or she is free to alter the dispositive scheme by the simple expedient of making a will.

There are only two limitations on the class of persons who may make a will. First, a testator must be at least eighteen years of age unless he or she is married or a member of the armed forces. Second, the testator must be of sound mind. The latter requirement does not refer to mental health or illness as a psychiatrist might classify it, but to testamentary capacity as defined by law. The testator must:

- understand the nature of the act of making a will
- know the nature and character of his or her property
- understand to whom he or she is giving his or her property
- understand the gifts he or she is making.

If these requirements are satisfied, it does not matter whether the testator is, medically speaking, suffering from mental illness, or whether he or she has been declared legally incompetent. One who suffers from such disabilities may execute a will during a "lucid interval" in which he or she meets the four-part test above.

There are three very different ways in which a valid will may be made. The most usual form of will is a document signed by the testator and two witnesses. The witnesses must be of sound mind, must be more than fourteen years old, and must sign in the presence of the testator. The witnesses need not, however, sign in each other's presence, nor need they be aware that they are witnessing a will.

A second form of valid will is the **holographic will**, which is a will written in the testator's handwriting and signed by the testator. All writing that is actually an essential part of the will must be in the testator's handwriting, but writing by others may be disregarded if it is not necessary to complete the will.

Finally, under very limited circumstances an oral or **nuncupative will** is valid. Such a will may apply only to personal property, must have been made during the testator's last sickness, must ordinarily be witnessed by three witnesses, and must ordinarily be probated within six months.

With limited exceptions, there are no restrictions on the manner in which property may be distributed by will. Among the few limitations is the **rule against perpetuities**, which has been previously discussed in connection with real property. In most jurisdictions following the common-law system of marital property, statutes provide that a surviving spouse may make an election between taking the share (if any) given him or her by the will and a share specified in the statute: these are known as **forced heirship statutes**.

In addition, common-law states give the widow **dower rights** in her husband's lands and the widower **curtesy rights** in his wife's lands. Community property states have no such provisions, and there is nothing to prevent one spouse from completely disinheriting the other. This is because half of the community property belongs to the spouse regardless of what the testator may do. A will that attempts to dispose of all of the community property, sometimes called a **widow's election will**, gives the survivor the option to take what the will gives him or her, or, alternatively to take his or her own half share of the community property irrespective of the will.

Problems may arise where the persons designated in the will to receive property (**devisees**, with respect to real property, and **legatees**, with respect to personal property) do not survive the testator. The common-law rule is that a testamentary gift to a person who is dead when the will takes effect "lapses," that is, disappears. This has been modified by statute in most states: if a child or other descendant predeceases the testator but leaves his or her own children or descendants, the gift to such beneficiary does not lapse but instead passes to the deceased beneficiary's children or descendants according to the rules of intestate succession.

The **Uniform Simultaneous Death Act** governs the situation in which the testator and beneficiary die so close together in time that it cannot be determined which died first, as in a plane crash or auto accident. In such a situation, half the property passes as though the testator had died first, and half as though the beneficiary had died first.

There are four basic classifications of legacies under a will. First is the **specific legacy** (or devise, when referring to real property). This is a testamentary gift of a specific object or tract of land, as "I give my gold watch to my son Bill.".

Next is the **demonstrative legacy**, which is a gift of a specified sum to be taken from a particular source, as "I give $10,000, to be taken from my Swiss bank account, to my wife Mary."

A **general legacy** is a gift out of the estate in general and not out of any specified fund or source, as "I give $500 to my servant Tom."

Finally, a **residuary legacy** is a gift of the balance of the testator's estate after all debts and other legacies have been paid, as "I give the balance of my estate, real and personal, to my husband George."

The importance of this classification is that certain priorities apply where the estate is not large enough to satisfy all debts and legacies. Debts are satisfied first, followed by specific, demonstrative, general, and residuary legacies, in that order. A specific legacy may also be **adeemed**, that is, destroyed, if the specific property in question is destroyed or sold before the testator's death. Thus in the example given, Bill would get nothing if the gold watch had been sold before the testator's death, while Mary would get $10,000 from other sources even if the Swiss bank account had been closed.

Finally, estate taxes are taken out of the residuary estate unless the will specifies otherwise, which may mean that most or all of the residuary legatees' share disappears in the payment of those taxes.

A will ordinarily remains in effect until revoked by the testator or by operation of law. While the making of a new will does not automatically revoke the old will unless the two wills are inconsistent, it is the usual practice to include in a new will a statement that the old will is revoked. Any document executed with the same formalities as are necessary to make a will may serve as a valid revocation.

A will may also be revoked by its physical mutilation or destruction by the testator or at the testator's direction and in his or her presence. Where a will is physically produced for probate, it is presumed until proven otherwise that it was not revoked. On the other hand, where a will was last seen in the testator's possession but cannot be found after the testator's death, or is found in a mutilated condition, it is presumed until proven otherwise that he or she revoked the will.

A will may also be revoked or partially revoked by operation of law. While a will is not revoked when the testator marries, it is revoked so far as the testator's spouse is concerned when the testator is divorced. The gift that would have been made to the divorced spouse passes instead as though the spouse had died before the testator. The **pretermitted child statute** operates with limited exceptions to revoke a will that was executed at a time when the testator had no living children if the testator later has a child who survives for one year after the testator's death. The statute also governs the case where a testator has children living at the time he or she makes a will but later has additional children; again, with limited exceptions, the new child is entitled to the share that the child would take by the intestate succession laws if the child is not otherwise provided for in the will.

A will that has been revoked can be revived only by reexecuting it just as though a new will were being made.

When a testator dies, his or her will must be **admitted to probate**, that is, filed in the probate court. A witnessed will may be admitted to probate upon the testimony of one of the attesting witnesses. If both witnesses are dead, the will may be proved by the testimony of two persons that the handwriting of the testator or of either witness is genuine.

Most modern wills contain a **self-proving affidavit**. If the self-proving affidavit is executed in a specified form by the testator and witnesses before a notary and is produced for probate (*i.e.*, where the will is lost), the execution of the will, the reason for its loss, and the contents of the will may be proved by testimony. A holographic will may be proved by the testimony of two witnesses that the will is in the testator's handwriting, or a self-proving affidavit by the testator (executed before a notary public) may be attached.

Once a will is admitted to probate, an **executor** is appointed to manage the estate. The will usually designates the executor, but if the will names no one, or if the executor dies or resigns, a statute provides priority for certain relatives or beneficiaries.

Most wills contain a clause providing for **independent administration**, whereby the executor may take charge of the estate on his or her own without court supervision. Independent administration is also available in limited circumstances where the testator has made no provision for it. Unless independent administration is obtained, all decisions relating to the estate (such as the sale of property, payment of debts, and distribution to the beneficiaries) must take place under the supervision of the probate court, often a very costly and time-consuming process.

No discussion of the law of wills would be complete without some reference to estate and inheritance taxes. A federal estate tax is imposed on all property remaining in an estate after debts have been paid, together with other property such as certain trust funds and property held in joint tenancy with right of survivorship. A deduction is allowed for property transferred to the decedent's spouse or to charity. The estate tax rates, like income tax rates, are graduated and depend on the size of the estate and the amount of property that has been transferred during the decedent's lifetime.

Gift taxes are also imposed in order to prevent evasion of estate taxes through lifetime gifts. It is the responsibility of the executor (called an administrator where the decedent dies without a will) to file the estate tax return within nine months of the decedent's death. Most states also impose an estate tax, which amount is usually determined by the credit for state estate taxes provided under the federal estate tax scheme. Some states also impose inheritance taxes, which are taxes on the beneficiaries and which depend on the amount of the inheritance and the relationship of the beneficiary to the deceased.

For more detailed information on wills and intestate succession, consult the Probate Code of your state or a treatise such as A. Casner, *Estate Planning*.

Having discussed the two principal branches of the law -- civil and criminal -- we now turn to topics of importance to all legal practitioners, regardless of their field of specialty. These include the rules of conduct by which all lawyers must abide (Chapter IV on Legal Ethics), the mechanics of determining the state of the law on a particular subject (Chapter V on Legal Research), and the jurisdiction, personnel, and procedure of the federal court system (Chapter VI).

TERMS TO KNOW

injunctions
common law
tort
battery
strictly liability torts
writ of trespass
tortfeasor
doctrine of transferred intent
assault
false imprisonment
intentional infliction of emotional distress
trespass
chattels
conversion
negligence
negligence per se
res ipsa loquitur
causation in fact
proximate causation
trespassers

attractive nuisance
licensees
invitees
comparative negligence
strict-liability torts
"one bite" rule
products liability
comparative causation
private nuisance
public nuisance
nuisance per se
deceit
fraud
business torts
negligent misrepresentation
interference with business relations
unfair competition
defamation
libel
slander
invasion of privacy
malicious prosecution
compensatory damages
punitive damages
exemplary damages
nominal damages
writ of assumpsit
Uniform Commercial Code
express contract
implied in fact
implied in law
quasi-contract liability
unjust enrichment
offer
acceptance
bilateral contract
unilateral contract
consideration
forbearance
promissory estoppel
detrimental reliance
parol evidence rule
Statute of Frauds
adhesion
duress
undue influence
intrinsic fraud
fraud in the factum
extrinsic fraud
fraud in the inducement
accord and satisfaction
novation
rescinded
specific performance
commercial paper
promissory notes
negotiable
negotiable instrument
secured transactions
security interest
lien
mortgage
tenant
estates in land
grantor
grantee
fee simple

fee simple subject to a condition subject
fee simple determinable
fee simple absolute
fee tail
life estate
estate pur autre vie
freehold estates
leasehold estates
term of years
periodic tenancy
tenancy at will
easement
utility easement
right of way easement
easement appurtenant
profits a prendre
licenses
restrictive covenants
tenancy in common
joint tenancy with right of survivorship
right of survivorship
tenancy by the entireties
remainder
mortgages
deeds of trust
liens
mortgagee
foreclosure
mortgagor
trustee
vendor's lien
mechanic's lien
materialsman's lien
tax liens
judgment lien
deed
livery of seisin
closing
general warranty deed
special warranty deed
quitclaim deed
clouds on the title
title search
abstract of title
title opinion
title insurance
bona fide purchaser
adverse possession
zoning ordinances
nonconforming uses
eminent domain
condemnation
equitable ownership
equitable conversion
trust
settlor
trustor
trustee
beneficiary
cestui que trust
revocable trust
irrevocable trust
inter vivos trust
testamentary trust
rule against perpetuities
quiet enjoyment
constructive eviction
assignment of the lease

sublease
forcible entry
ejectment
forcible entry and detainer
heirs
escheat
testator
intestate succession
per capita
per stirpes
holographic will
nuncupative will
forced heirship statutes
dower rights
curtesy rights
widow's election will
devisees
legatees
Uniform Simultaneous
  Death Act
specific legacy
demonstrative legacy
general legacy
residuary legacy
adeemed
pretermitted child statute
self-proving affidavit
executor
independent administration

FOOTNOTES

1. See *Weigel v. McCloskey*, 113 Ark. 1, 166 S.W. 944 (1914).
2. For an example of such a case, see *Hill v. Kimball*, 76 Tex. 210, 13 S.W. 59 (1890).
3. 24 Vand. L. Rev. 1133 (1971).
4. See *Martin v. Herzog*, 228 N.Y. 164, 126 N.E. 814 (1920).

5. See *Byrne v. Boadle*, 2 H. & C. 722, 159 Eng. Rep. 299 (1863).

6. Compare *In re Kinsman Transit Co.*, 338 F.2d 708 (2d Cir. 1964) with *In re Kinsman Transit Co.*, 388 F.2d 821 (2d Cir. 1968).

7. See *Kimble v. Mackintosh Hemphill Co.*, 359 Pa. 461, 59 A.2d 68 (1948).

8. See *Lemon v. Edwards*, 344 S.W. 2d 822 (Ky. 1961).

9. See *McCullough v. Beech Aircraft Corp.*, 587 F.2d 754 (5th Cir. 1979).

10. See *Foster v. Ford Motor Co.*, 621 F.2d 715 (5th Cir. 1980).

11. See *Signal Oil & Gas Co. v. Universal Oil Products*, 572 S.W.2d 320 (Tex. 1978).

12. See *Culwell v. Abbott Construction Co.*, 211 Kan. 359, 506 P.2d 1191 (1973).

13. See *Village of Euclid v. Ambler Realty Co.*, 272 U.S. 365. 368 (1926).

14. Uniform Commercial Code, §2-305.

15. See *Cotnam v. Wisdom*, 83 Ark. 601, 104 S.W. 164 (1907).

16. Uniform Commercial Code, §2-205.

17. See *Hamer v. Sidway*, 124 N.Y. 538, 27 N.E. 256 (1891).

18. Uniform Commercial Code, §2-202.

19. 79 U.S. (12 Wall.) 443, 445 (1870).

20. See also Uniform Commercial Code, §2-302.

21. See *Mitchell v. C.C. Sanitation Co.*, 430 S.W.2d 933 (Tex Civ. App. -- Houston [14th Dist.] 1968, writ ref'd n.r.e.

22. See *Methodist Mission Home v. B.*, 451 S.W.2d 539 (Tex. Civ. App. – San Antonio 1970, no writ).

23. See *Village of Euclid v. Ambler Realty Co.*, 272 U.S. 365 (1926, which sustained the constitutionality of so-called "Euclidean" zoning, whereby zones of land with fixed boundaries are designated for specific uses.

24. See *Lucas v. Hamm*, 56 Cal. Rptr. 821 P.2d 685 (1961).

25. 430 U.S. 672 (1977).

CHAPTER IV

LEGAL ETHICS

The practice of law, like the practice of medicine and other learned professions, is regulated by each of the fifty states. This regulation takes two principal forms: restrictions on who may practice law, and restrictions on the manner in which it may be practiced. Each of these types of regulation is important to the legal assistant. In a recent American Bar Association Formal Opinion, the Standing Committee on Professional Ethics stated:

> A lawyer can employ lay secretaries, lay investigators, lay detectives, lay researchers, and lay scriveners. In fact, he may employ nonlawyers to do any task for him except counsel clients about law matters, engage directly in the practice of law, appear in court or appear in formal proceedings. . . so long as it is he who takes the work and vouches for it to the client and becomes responsible for it to the client. In other words, we do not limit the kind of assistance that a lawyer can acquire in any way . . . so long as the nonlawyers do not do things that lawyers may not do or do the things that lawyers only may do.[1]

Thus legal assistants must refrain from activities which constitute the actual practice of law and must be careful to observe the same standards of ethical conduct that are applicable to the lawyers for whom they work.

Admission to the Bar is controlled in each state by the legislature or Supreme Court of that state, often through a Board of Bar Examiners composed of lawyers from throughout the state. With rare exceptions, all applicants for the Bar must be graduates of a law school accredited by the American Bar Association. Most states also require at least some college-level training. Applicants must pass a bar examination consisting of multiple-choice questions in areas of the law common to all states and essay questions on the law of the state in which they seek to be licensed. Applicants who pass the bar exam must take an oath and, in many states, must pay annual dues to the State Bar Association as a condition of retaining their licenses.

What, then, are the activities in which only lawyers may engage? The answer to this question is not a simple one: one court has referred to "the line of demarcation, often shadowy and wavering, which defines the limits of the functions of the legal adviser from those of the layman."[2] Nevertheless, it is possible to identify a number of activities that most or all states agree constitute the practice of law in most or all circumstances.

Some of these are suggested by the above-quoted Bar Association Opinion: a nonlawyer may not:

- give advice to clients concerning their legal rights and responsibilities;
- hold himself or herself out to the public as a lawyer;
- appear as the legal representative of a client before a court.

Other, less obvious prohibitions are also present. For example, a nonlawyer may not use a lawyer's professional stationery without in some manner identifying himself or herself as a nonlawyer (*e.g.*. "Dana Doe, Legal Assistant"). To do otherwise might mislead the recipient as to the nonlawyer's status.[3]

Finally, except as part of a retirement plan, a nonlawyer may not share in the profits of a lawyer's practice and may not participate in the management of a law firm.[4]

With these principal exceptions, a legal assistant may do anything that a lawyer may do. The legal assistant's activities are, however, undertaken as the agent of the lawyer and under the lawyer's supervision.[5] The lawyer must maintain a direct relationship with the client, supervise the delegated work, and have complete responsibility for the work product. This includes both the accuracy of the legal assistant's work and the propriety of the legal assistant's conduct. Thus, the legal assistant has a responsibility to his or her employer to ensure that the legal assistant's job is performed competently and ethically, since the lawyer as well as the legal assistant will bear responsibility for any shortcomings.

If legal assistants may assume a wide range of responsibilities, what are the ethical obligations that accompany those responsibilities? At a minimum, the legal assistant must bear the same ethical responsibilities as the lawyer for whom he or she works. In the words of Opinion 316, "nonlawyers may not do things that lawyers may not do."

The ethical responsibilities of attorneys are established in each state by the legislature of Supreme Court of the state. The ethical codes of most states are based, sometimes with minor modifications, on the Code of Professional Responsibility of the American Bar Association adopted by that organization in 1969. The standards of legal ethics are the subject of constant reevaluation. The 1969 Code was based in large part on thirty-two Canons of Professional Ethics adopted by the ABA in 1908 and on fifteen additional Canons adopted between 1928 and 1937.

The ABA has adopted Model Rules of Professional Conduct as the standard of professional conduct for attorneys throughout the country. Through its Standing Committee on Ethics and Professional Responsibility, the ABA also issues formal and informal opinions on questions of legal ethics submitted to it by attorneys. State and local bar associations often issue similar opinions.

The ABA Code of Professional Responsibility consists of:

- Canons that express "in general terms the standards of professional conduct expected of lawyers in their relationships with the public, with the legal system and with the legal profession"

- Ethical Considerations, which "represent the objectives toward which every lawyer should strive" and which "constitute a body of principles upon which the lawyer can rely for guidance in many specific situations"

- Disciplinary Rules, mandatory in character, which "state the minimum level of conduct below which no lawyer can fall without being subject to disciplinary action."

Some aspects of the Code will have little applicability to legal assistants. What follows is a discussion of some of those features of which legal assistants should be aware in their day-to-day work.

Canon 1 states that "[a] lawyer should assist in maintaining the integrity and competence of the legal profession." In particular, attorneys must not engage in:

- illegal conduct
- conduct involving dishonesty, fraud, deceit, or misrepresentation
- conduct that is prejudicial to the administration of justice
- conduct that adversely reflects on their fitness to practice law.

Lawyers must not violate the disciplinary rules, nor may they circumvent the disciplinary rules through the actions of others. An attorney should not advise or sanction an act by his or her client that the attorney should not do.[6]

An attorney who becomes aware of improper conduct by another attorney must report such conduct to the appropriate authorities. Likewise, attorneys must cooperate with disciplinary investigations of other attorneys.

Canon 2 states that "[a] lawyer should assist the legal profession in fulfilling its duty to make legal counsel available." Topics under this Canon include publicity and advertising by lawyers, solicitation of legal business, specialization, fees and fee-splitting, and acceptance of and withdrawal from legal employment. While these topics are not of direct concern to the legal assistant, he or she should be aware of the basic guidelines in these areas as part of a general understanding of legal ethics.

The rules concerning lawyer advertising are at present in a state of flux. Prior to 1977, virtually all publicity and advertising by lawyers was prohibited. In that year, however, the United States Supreme Court held in the case of *Bates v. State Bar of Arizona*[7] that lawyer advertising was protected in large part by the First Amendment.

In contrast, the ABA Model Rules of Professional Conduct place few restrictions on lawyer advertising, so long as it is not false, fraudulent, or misleading. Future rules in this area are likely to fall somewhere between these two extremes.

Solicitation of clients to obtain their legal business is regulated by Disciplinary Rules 2-103 and 2-104. In essence these rules provide that a lawyer may not recommend himself or herself to a person who has not sought the lawyer's advice and may not accept employment from a person to whom he or she has given unsolicited advice except where the person is a relative, close friend, or former or current client. A lawyer may not request a person or organization to recommend his or her services or to contact a prospective client on the lawyer's behalf, nor may the lawyer reward someone for doing so.

The rules concerning solicitation, like those concerning advertising, are undergoing rapid change. In 1978 the Supreme Court held in *In re Primus*[8] that some solicitation is constitutionally protected, but also held in *Ohralik v. Ohio State Bar Association*[9] that some forms of solicitation are not protected. The ABA Model Rules permit solicitation only under limited circumstances and prohibit coercion, duress, harassment, and taking advantage of the client's physical, emotional, or mental state.[10]

With the exception of patent, trademark, and admiralty attorneys, lawyers may not refer to themselves as specialists in a particular field of law unless they are certified as specialists by their state board of legal specialization. In some states, lawyers who meet certain experience and education requirements and who pass an examination may be certified as specialists in areas offered by their state's board of legal specialization.

The fees charged by a lawyer must be reasonable and should be explained to the client in advance. Some of the factors that should be considered in determining a reasonable fee include:

- the time, labor, and skill required to perform the legal service properly
- the novelty and difficulty of the questions involved
- the customary fee of other lawyers for the same services
- the amount involved and the results obtained
- the experience, reputation, and ability of the lawyer involved.

In most civil cases, lawyers may charge a contingency fee, that is, a fee (usually a percentage of the amount recovered) that is to be paid by the client only if the case is successful.

A fee may be divided among lawyers who are not part of the same firm only where the client consents and where the total fee is reasonable. A few states permit a lawyer who "forwards" a case to another lawyer to collect a fee for that service.

It has been a longstanding tradition of the Bar that lawyers often represent charitable organizations or those who are unable to afford necessary legal services at no charge or at a reduced charge. This service, together with participation in activities for improving the law, the legal system, or the legal profession, is referred to as "*pro bono publico*" or "*pro bono*" service.

The issue of mandatory "pro bono" is an ongoing topic of discussion.

More legal assistants are accepting the responsibility for *pro bono* services by volunteering in legal clinics, courts, and mediation services. *Pro bono* offers the legal assistant the opportunity to learn a field of law in which he or she does not work on a daily basis.

While the standards governing acceptance of employment are very broad, the circumstances under which a lawyer may discontinue representation are carefully regulated. A lawyer must withdraw if:

- the client insists that the lawyer pursue a course or action solely for purposes of harassment
- the lawyer will be forced to violate a Disciplinary Rule
- the lawyer is unable to continue effective representation
- the lawyer is discharged by the client.

A lawyer may withdraw under a variety of other circumstances, so long as he or she takes all reasonable steps to avoid prejudice to the rights of his or her client. The lawyer must give due notice to the client, allowing time for employment of other counsel, and must deliver to the client all papers and property to which the client is entitled, including a refund of any unearned fees. In most circumstances, permission of the court is required for a lawyer to withdraw from a pending lawsuit, and the lawyer must continue representation if ordered to do so by the court.

Under Canon 3, "[a] lawyer should assist in preventing the unauthorized practice of law." There is a fine line between those activities that constitute the practice of law and those that do not, and this aspect of Canon 3 has been discussed in general terms above. Canon 3 also prohibits a lawyer from sharing legal fees with nonlawyers, except through retirement plans or through payments to the estate of a deceased lawyer. Likewise, a law partnership may not include a nonlawyer as a partner.

Canon 4 states that "[a] lawyer should preserve the confidences and secrets of a client." The information covered by this Canon falls into two categories:

- information protected by the attorney/client privilege, that is, information that may be legally withheld from evidence in a court of law ("**confidences**").

- other information gained in the professional relationship that the client has requested to be kept secret, the disclosure of which would be embarrassing or potentially detrimental to the client ("**secrets**").

The attorney/client privilege is governed by state and federal law and not by standards of legal ethics. In order to be privileged, however, a statement must be made outside the presence of anyone except the attorney and the attorney's legal assistants, secretaries, investigators, or other agents. The client may, of course, waive this right if he or she so chooses, thereby permitting the lawyer to make the disclosure. Federal Rule of Evidence 501 makes a state's rule applicable in federal cases with respect to questions governed by state law.

Confidential information may be revealed with the consent of the client (or all the clients, if the information relates to more than one client), but only after a full disclosure of all the relevant factors. Confidential information may also be revealed when required by law or court order or when necessary to prevent the client from committing a crime. The Model Rules limit such disclosure to crimes involving death or serious bodily harm.

Finally, a lawyer may reveal confidential information to establish or collect his or her fee or to defend himself, herself or his or her employees or associates against an accusation of wrongful conduct, but only when it is necessary to do so.[11]

The obligation of confidentiality is especially important for the legal assistant. The operation of a successful law practice requires that clients' confidential information be shared among lawyers within the firm and with legal assistants and other support personnel, and there is nothing unethical about such disclosure. It is extremely important, however, that those to whom confidential information is revealed treat that information in the same manner as is required of the attorney handling the case.

An attorney is responsible for improper disclosure by the attorney's employees. Disciplinary Rule 4-101 (D) states that "[a] lawyer shall exercise reasonable care to prevent his employees, associates, and others whose services are utilized by him from disclosing or using confidences or secrets of a client. . ."

Clients are protected from conflicts of interest on the part of their lawyers by Canon 5, which states that "[a] lawyer should exercise independent professional judgment on behalf of a client." Under this Canon, a lawyer must not accept employment in cases where the lawyer's judgment may be affected by his or her own financial, business, property, or personal interests, except with the consent of the client after full disclosure. Thus, for example, a lawyer may not prepare an instrument, such as a will, giving the lawyer or a member of the lawyer's family a gift. By the same token, a lawyer must not obtain any ownership interest in his or her client's case (except for a contingent fee arrangement or a lien to secure the lawyer's fee and expenses), since to do so might affect the lawyer's judgment as to the client's best interests. A lawyer should not make loans to a client in connection with litigation, except that the lawyer may prepay expenses on behalf of the client.

Finally, a lawyer must not enter into a business transaction with a client except under limited circumstances designed to ensure that the transaction is fair and equitable to the client. In this regard, a lawyer may not acquire publication rights with respect to a client's case until that case is concluded.

Conflicts of interest may also arise due to a lawyer's representation of other clients. For this reason, a lawyer must not accept employment from a client if the lawyer's professional judgment on behalf of other clients will be impaired. A lawyer may represent clients with conflicting interests only if *both* clients, after disclosure of all the facts and circumstances, consent. If a conflict arises between two clients in the course of their representation, the lawyer must resolve the conflict by withdrawing from one or both cases.

A lawyer may not make an aggregate settlement of the claims for or against two or more of his clients unless the terms are fully disclosed to the clients and each consents.

A lawyer is often asked to serve as an intermediary between clients. For example, a lawyer may be asked by a husband and wife who have been previous clients to arrange the terms of an uncontested divorce settlement. Under the Model Rules, a lawyer may participate in such an arrangement only under limited circumstances. Each client must be able to make informed decisions; the lawyer must be able to act impartially and without prejudice to the clients' interests; and each client must consent after an understanding of the advantages and risks of such an arrangement. A lawyer must withdraw from such representation on the request of either client or if it becomes apparent that genuine conflict has arisen.

Under limited circumstances, a lawyer may accept compensation for his or her services from someone other than the client. Thus, for example, a lawyer may be paid by a liability insurance carrier to represent a customer of the carrier who is being sued. Full disclosure to the client must be made, and an arrangement must be provided that insures that the lawyer can exercise independent professional judgment on behalf of the client.

A lawyer must not accept or continue representation:

- where it is apparent that the lawyer will be a witness, except where the testimony relates to an uncontested matter or formality;
- where the testimony relates to the lawyer's fee; and
- where refusal or withdrawal would work a substantial hardship on the client.

Under the Model Rules members of a lawyer's firm may testify if no conflict of interest is created.

Canon 6 states that "[a] lawyer should represent a client competently." The requirements of this Canon are simple: a lawyer must not handle a matter that he or she is not competent to handle, unless the lawyer undertakes the work and study necessary to qualify himself or herself. A lawyer must not handle a matter without adequate preparation and must not neglect a matter entrusted to him or her. These obligations include:

- prompt attention to legal matters
- adequate communication with clients
- punctuality in appearances before courts
- adequate continuing legal education.

While the requirement that a lawyer be competent ought to be self-evident, the fact is that neglect and inadequate representation are a major disciplinary problem. Federal Judge Jerry Buchmeyer has estimated that over 1/3 of all grievances filed against Texas attorneys relate to such problems.[12]

Canon 7, which provides that "[a] lawyer should represent a client zealously within the bounds of the law," is by far the most complex of the Canons. The Ethical Considerations and Disciplinary Rules under this Canon attempt to balance the lawyer's duty to be a vigorous advocate for his or her client's interests with the lawyer's duty to be fair and honest with the legal system and with opposing parties and counsel.

A lawyer must seek the lawful objectives of his or her client through all reasonably available means permitted by law and the standards of legal ethics. A lawyer's personal distaste for a client, or disagreement with the client's conduct or legal position, does not affect the lawyer's obligation to represent the client to the best of the lawyer's ability. Under our legal system, individuals are generally permitted, within the bounds of the law, to decide for themselves whether their conduct is appropriate or inappropriate, and it is for the courts and not for attorneys to decide whether a particular course of conduct is legally permissible. This does not mean that the lawyer may not urge a client to do what the lawyer thinks is right, but the final decision must be the client's.[13]

The lawyer's obligation to represent his or her client zealously is not absolute and must yield to a duty of fairness, honesty, and courtesy. A lawyer must always be courteous to the courts and to opposing parties and counsel and should agree to reasonable requests regarding court proceedings, settings, continuances, waiver of procedural formalities, and similar matters that do not prejudice the rights of the lawyer's client. The lawyer should generally comply with local customs of courtesy or practice of the Bar or of a particular court. A lawyer must not take any action solely for purposes of harassment or delay, make any frivolous legal argument, make any misrepresentation of law or fact, or create, preserve, or use false evidence.

A lawyer who becomes aware of fraud committed by a person who is not the lawyer's client must promptly reveal the fraud. The duty of the lawyer to reveal his or her own client's fraud is an area of legal ethics that is undergoing continuing debate. The Model Rules contain a requirement applicable in civil cases that the lawyer must call upon his or her client to rectify the fraud. If the client fails to do so, the lawyer must reveal the fraud.

The area of greatest concern involves a lawyer whose client wishes to commit perjury in the course of a criminal trial. Special standards adopted by the American Bar Association in 1969 require that the lawyer in such a situation withdraw if possible. If withdrawal is impossible, the lawyer must allow the client to tell the client's perjurious story without benefit of direct questioning by the lawyer and without the lawyer's referring to the false testimony in closing argument.[14]

The Model Rules take the position that a lawyer may not participate in perjurious testimony and must reveal perjury when it occurs.[15]

A lawyer may not communicate directly with an opposing party whom the lawyer knows to be represented by counsel without the permission of that person's lawyer, nor may the lawyer cause another person to make such contact. In particular, a lawyer may not engage in settlement negotiations with an opposing party without the consent of that party's counsel.[16] A lawyer may not give legal advice to an opposing party who is not represented by a lawyer, except for the advice to secure a lawyer.

A lawyer may not make or threaten to make a criminal charge against someone solely to obtain an advantage in a civil case.

In presenting a case, a lawyer may not:

- refer to irrelevant matters or matters not supported by evidence
- ask degrading questions that are not relevant to the case
- state his or her personal knowledge of the facts or his or her personal opinion regarding the matters in question.

The Model Rules provide elaborate guidelines concerning public statements that a lawyer may make concerning pending litigation. These guidelines are designed to ensure that civil or criminal proceedings are not influenced by reports in the press. Disciplinary Rule 7-107(J) requires a lawyer to exercise reasonable care to prevent the lawyer's employees from making statements that the lawyer is prohibited from making.

A lawyer may not contact prospective or actual jurors or their families before or during the course of a lawsuit or criminal trial. After the case is concluded and the jury is discharged, the ethical standards prohibit a lawyer from contacting a juror or the juror's family solely for purposes of harassment or embarrassment. It should be noted that the rules of some courts prohibit all contact with jurors after a trial except by permission of the court.

Finally, a lawyer must report improper conduct by jurors or improper contact by anyone with a juror or member of the juror's family.

A lawyer may not advise or cause a person to hide himself or herself or to leave the jurisdiction for the purpose of making himself or herself unavailable as a witness. A lawyer may pay an expert witness a reasonable fee for the expert witness' services but may pay a non-expert witness only for the expenses and loss of time incurred by such non-expert witness in attending or testifying. In no case may a witness be paid a contingency fee.

A lawyer must not make gifts or loans to any judge or judicial employee. A lawyer may not communicate with a judge except during the course of court proceedings or when the opposing party or attorney is present. The opposing party or attorney must be furnished with a copy of any written communications to the judge.

Canon 8, which states that "[a] lawyer should assist in improving the legal system," regulates the conduct of lawyers who are public officials or judicial candidates. The canon prohibits lawyers from making false accusations against a judge.

Canon 9 states that "[a] lawyer should avoid even the appearance of professional impropriety." This Canon governs conduct that is not necessarily improper by itself but that is likely to create the appearance of impropriety and hence to reflect badly on the lawyer and legal system.

In addition to this general standard, there are some specific prohibitions under Canon 9. Lawyers are prohibited from accepting private employment in matters with which they have dealt as a judge or public employee. A lawyer may not state or imply that he or she is able to improperly influence any tribunal, legislative body, or public official.

Disciplinary Rule 9-102 governs a lawyer's handling of the funds and property of the lawyer's clients. Such funds must be placed in a separate bank account or accounts and may not be commingled with funds of the lawyer. A lawyer must promptly notify a client of the receipt of funds or other property, must maintain complete records of such funds or property, and must promptly deliver the funds to the client upon request.

Many of the foregoing standards of legal ethics will have little relevance to the legal assistant. Some, however, are of crucial importance. The legal assistant should particularly be aware of Disciplinary Rule 5.3, which clearly obligates the attorney to supervise all work by a non-attorney.

In addition, these topics will play a significant role in the day-to-day work of the legal assistant:

- Publicity, Advertising, and Solicitation
  - Old ABA Canon 27
  - Disciplinary Rules 2-101 through 2-104
  - Model Rules 7.1 through 7.5

- Unauthorized Practice
  - Old ABA Canon 47
  - Disciplinary Rule 3-101
  - Model Rule 7.4(c)

- Sharing Fees with Nonlawyers
  - Old ABA Canon 34
  - Disciplinary Rule 3-102)

- Confidential Communications
  - Old ABA Canon 37
  - Disciplinary Rule 4-101
  - Model Rule 1.6

- Competence
  - Old ABA Canon 21
  - Disciplinary Rule 6-101
  - Model Rule 1.1

- Communication with Adverse Party
  - Old ABA Canon 9
  - Disciplinary Rule 7-104
  - Model Rules 4.2 and 4.3

- Trial Publicity
  - Old ABA Canon 20
  - Disciplinary Rule 7-108
  - Model Rule 3.6

- Contact with Jurors

  - Old ABA Canon 23
  - Disciplinary Rule 7-108
  - Model Rule 3.5

- Contact with Witnesses
  - Old ABA Canons 18 and 39
  - Disciplinary Rule 7-109
  - Model Rule 3.4

- Contact with Officials
  - Old ABA Canon 3
  - Disciplinary Rule 7-110
  - Model Rule 3.5

While these are the topics most directly relevant to the work of a legal assistant, he or she must be generally familiar with all the standards of legal ethics.

There are at least two reasons why this is the case:

- the legal assistant must be careful to avoid deliberately or accidentally violating any of these standards or causing his or her employer to violate the standards

- it is the legal assistant's obligation, just as it is the lawyer's, to report any substantial violation of the standards.

The descriptions of ethical standards in this chapter are only summaries. Most of the standards have been over-simplified, and many of the more detailed points have been omitted. Whenever the legal assistant is in need of the precise ethical standards applicable in a particular situation, he or she should directly consult the state's Rules of Professional Conduct. The Model Rules of Professional Conduct may be found in the November 1982 issue of the American Bar Association *Journal*. Summaries of current opinions of the ABA Standing Committee on Ethics and Professional Responsibility are published from time to time in the American Bar Association *Journal*. Other publications on the subject of legal ethics may be found in any good law library.

TERMS TO KNOW

confidences
secrets

FOOTNOTES

1. ABA Formal Opinion 316 (1967).
2. *State ex re. Johnson v. Childe*. 139 Neb. 91, 95, 295 N.W. 381, 384 (1941).
3. ABA Informal Opinion 660.
4. ABA Formal Opinion 303 (1961).
5. ABA Formal Opinion 85 (1932).
6. ABA Formal Opinion 75 (1932).
7. 433 U.S. 350 (1977).
8. 436 U.S. 412 (1978).
9. 436 U.S. 447 (1978).
10. Model Rule 7.3.
11. ABA Formal Opinion 19 (1930).
12. Buchmeyer, *How to Avoid Grievance Complaints*, 43 Tex. B.J. 113 (1980).
13. Model Rule 2.1.
14. *ABA Project on Standards of Criminal Justice: The Defense Function* §7.7 (1969).
15. Model Rule 3.3.
16. ABA Formal Opinion 124 (1934).

CHAPTER V

LEGAL RESEARCH

The public often imagines that a lawyer has the answer to every legal question -- or at least every legal question within the lawyer's area of specialization -- at his or her fingertips. When confronted with a legal problem, they expect a lawyer to think back to his or her law school training and immediately arrive at the correct and complete answer.

Unfortunately for the legal profession (but perhaps fortunately for the legal publishing industry), matters are seldom that simple. The amount of substantive and procedural law in any given jurisdiction is far beyond the capacity of any lawyer to learn and remember. Even in a given specialty, the most that can be expected is that a lawyer will master the basic rules and be familiar with the most fundamental cases and statutes that govern the lawyer's practice.

The lawyer may face a question involving the law of a foreign country or of a state other than the lawyer's own. Not even the most brilliant legal scholar can be familiar with such a vast body of material.

Finally, new cases are being decided and new statutes, regulations, and rulings passed every day. It is impossible to keep up with this influx of new law in its entirety.

For all these reasons, **legal research**, the process of looking up the law on a particular topic, is a basic part of the training of every legal professional.

Even if one were somewhere to find the mythical lawyer who knew all the answers to all the questions, legal research would still be necessary. Successful legal argument, both oral and written, depends not only on knowing the answers, but on being able to convince the judge or judges that the answers put forth by the lawyer are indeed correct. This is accomplished by the **citation** of relevant legal materials in support of the lawyer's contentions. The judge or the judge's staff can then refer to these materials to ascertain whether or not the lawyer has correctly interpreted and is correctly stating the rules of law that the materials contain.

Knowing the relevant law is important, but being able to demonstrate the state of the law is often equally important. Only lawyers can argue in court and provide legal advice to clients, but a properly trained legal assistant can be an invaluable aid in helping the lawyer learn and demonstrate the law.

The questions that must be answered can range from the simple and straightforward ("What is the statute of limitations for burglary?") to the complex, difficult, and sometimes unanswerable. ("How have the courts interpreted the phrase 'actual cash value' as used in insurance policies in connection with the loss of men's clothing samples?")

Regardless of the nature of the problem, however, or its degree of difficulty, there are certain fundamental techniques of legal research that will lead the researcher to the correct answer, or, sometimes of equal importance, demonstrate that the problem is one that has never before been addressed by the law. Mastery of legal research requires three types of knowledge:

- an understanding of the sources from which various types of law are derived

- familiarity with the legal materials in which law from each of these sources is embodied
- a systematic way of using these materials to locate the answer to a given question.

Sources of the Law.

The three main sources of law in the United States correspond to our three branches of government: executive, legislative, and judicial.

Since the courts are the ultimate arbiters of the law, the law made by the judicial branch is often of greatest importance to the legal researcher. The decisions rendered by judges over the years are relevant to current legal problems through the doctrine of **stare decisis** (Latin for "let the decision stand"). In order to maintain consistency, fairness, and economy of effort, a rule of law established in one case (a **precedent**) is followed in similar cases as they arise, unless the court is firmly convinced that the rule is incorrect or unless changing circumstances have rendered the rule no longer equitable.

Although some judicial decisions, especially at the trial court level, are announced orally, these decisions lack permanence and widespread availability and are therefore seldom of much use to the legal researcher. Of far greater value are the written opinions of appellate courts and some trial courts that are reported and published nationwide.

A judicial opinion will not only state the outcome of the case before the court but will explain the facts of the case, the court's reasoning, and precedent on which the court relies in reaching its decision. This gives the opinion particular value to the legal researcher. The facts stated in the opinion can be compared to the facts of the problem at hand; the court's reasoning can be examined to determine whether it is persuasive and logical; and the precedents cited by the court can be checked to determine whether they are themselves of assistance.

Reported judicial decisions form by far the largest body of written law. There are presently over 3,000,000 reported cases, and dozens of volumes of new opinions are issued every year.

The role of the legislative branch in the establishment of law has grown enormously in modern times. In ancient England and in colonial America, **statutes** were the exception rather than the rule, and were enacted only where the **common law** failed to supply the answer or reached an unsatisfactory result.

Today the tables have been turned. Most modern judicial decisions "fill in the gaps" in the text of statutory enactments. Indeed, it is becoming increasingly difficult to find a legal subject on which the federal or state legislatures, or both, have not passed legislation.

Where a statute is plain and specific, its text is often the only legislative source to which the researcher need refer. There can be little doubt about the meaning of a statute that states, for example, that "Rhode Island constitutes one judicial district. Court shall be held at Providence."[1] Other statutes, however, can be considerably more vague. How, for example, should the courts interpret a statute which states that "[e]very contract, combination in the form of trust or otherwise, or conspiracy in restraint of trade or commerce . . . is declared illegal?"[2]

Where the text of a statute is vague or ambiguous, its **legislative history** can sometimes furnish the necessary clarification. The legislative history of a statute includes:

- the record of its passage through the legislature
- prior drafts of the statute
- transcripts of the hearings of committees to which the proposed statute was referred
- reports of those committees recommending that the statute be passed, often proposing amendments
- the debates about the statute on the floor of the legislature
- (sometimes) the speeches made by the chief executive signing the statute into law.

Of increasing importance in recent years is the law made by the executive branch of government. Administrative agencies and officers of the executive branch often exercise a quasi-legislative function, adopting regulations that have the force of law. These regulations, issued pursuant to authority delegated by the legislature, may interpret a statute, providing answers to detailed questions where the statute speaks only in generalities, or may establish rules of procedure for implementing the statute.

Some regulations affect only the conduct of the agency itself (such as a regulation establishing an agency's hours of business), while others require affirmative conduct by private individuals or corporations (such as regulations requiring certain safety devices or warnings in hazardous places of employment).

Executive agencies and officers may also perform a quasi-judicial function. Each year agencies such as the Federal Trade

Commission and the Federal Energy Regulatory Commission issue thousands of rulings in administrative proceedings that come before them, often issuing written opinions that resemble judicial opinions. Officials such as attorneys general, state comptrollers, and representatives of the Internal Revenue Service also issue opinions on matters referred to them by other officials and by private parties.

Finally, strange as it may seem, some sources of law are not associated with government. While the statement or action of an individual or group with the power to make the law, such as a judge, legislature, agency, or official, provides direct guidance to the legal researcher, the opinion of someone particularly qualified to analyze, predict, or recommend the law is also of value in answering legal questions. Such a person may be a distinguished lawyer, a law professor, a retired or active judge, or simply an author in a prestigious legal periodical or other well-regarded legal publication.

Where an opinion is put forth by such a person, it often carries the weight of law, since it is likely to be followed by courts, legislators, and other lawmakers. These so-called **secondary sources** include such items as legal encyclopedias, law reviews, legal treatises, and form books.

Legal Materials.

Having identified the sources of the law, we must now explore the variety of legal materials in which that law is located. Each source of law is associated with several types of legal materials in which its output is published. In addition, some types of legal materials do not directly present the law but operate as research aids to facilitate the use of other materials.

Judicial decisions are collected and published in volumes known as **reporters**. Some state courts and the United States Supreme Court have **official reporters** issued by the government, in which those courts' decisions are published.

Most federal courts and an increasing number of state courts have no official reporter. For these courts, **unofficial reporters**, published by a private legal publishing company, are the means by which opinions are disseminated. The unofficial reporters also provide a handy reprint of officially reported decisions.

The accompanying chart summarizes the reporters that publish the decisions of the various American courts. Each type of federal court has its own reporter system. Selected decisions of the United States District Courts are published in the *Federal Supplement* or the *Federal Rules Decisions*. Opinions of the United States Courts of Appeals are reported in the *Federal Reporter*. The United States Supreme Court has an official reporter (the *United States Reports*) and two permanent unofficial reporters (the *Supreme Court Reporter* and *United States Supreme Court Reports - Lawyers' Edition*).

While a few states still publish official reporters for their courts, most states have eliminated such reporters as a cost-saving measure and instead rely upon the National Reporter System, published by the West Publishing Company of St. Paul, Minnesota.

JURISDICTION & COURT	REPORTER (S) AND SAMPLE CITATION (S)	DIGESTS	SHEPARD'S	LEGISLATIVE MATERIALS	ADMINISTRATIVE MATERIALS
United States Supreme Court	United States Reports* (407 U.S. 389 (1980)) (including slip opinions) Supreme Court Reporter (99 S. St. 406 (1980)) Lawyers' Edition (66 L. Ed. 2d 147 (1980)) U.S. Law Week (49 U.S.L.W. 4063 (1980))	Supreme Court Digest Federal Practice Digest 2d Modern Federal Practice Digest	United States Citations	*Codes:* United States Code (28 U.S.C. § 1332) United States Code Annotated (28 U.S.C.A. § 1332) *Session Laws:* Statutes at Large (41 Stat. 712 (1980)) Slip Laws *Legislative History:* Committee Hearings Committee Reports U.S. Code Congressional & Administrative News (1980 U.S. Code Cong. & Ad. News 3412) Congressional Record (37 Cong. Rec. 32,451 (1980))	*Codes:* Code of Federal Regulations (29 C.F.R. § 17.01 (c)) *Registers:* Federal Register (67 Fed. Reg. 34,249 (1980)) *Decisions:* Specialized Reporters, such as Federal Trade Commission Decisions (56 F.T.C. 203 1980))
United States Courts of Appeals	Federal Reporter (621 F. 2d 149 (5th Cir. 1980)) (slip opinions for some circuits, including Fifth)	Federal Practice Digest 2d Modern Federal Practice Digest	Federal Citations Part I		
United States District Courts	Federal Supplement (574 F. Supp. 37 (E.D. Wisconsin 1983)) Federal Rules Decisions (104 F.R.D. 136 (D. Maine 1985)) Federal Reporter (very early cases only)	Same	Federal Citations Part II		
State Supreme Courts	Sometimes an official reporter, such as Hawaii Reports* (241 Haw. 301 (1962)) National Reporter System, such as Pacific Reporter (675 P. 2d 9 (Colo. 1984))	State Digests, such as Pennsylvania Digest Regional Digests, such as Atlantic Digest Barclays' California Law Monthly	State citators, such as Indiana Citations Regional citators, such as Southwestern Citations	*Codes:* General codes, such as Equity's New Hampshire Revised Statutes Annotated (N.H. Rev. Civ. Stat. Ann. art. 226) Subject-matter codes, such as West's California Legislative Service *Session Laws:* Individual state session laws, such as Nebraska Laws (1973 Neb. Laws 1547 (1973)) Usually no slip laws *Legislative History:* Usually none	*Codes:* Individual state codes *Registers:* Individual state registers, such as Florida Administrative Register *Decisions:* Occasionally a specialized reporter
Intermediate State Appellate Courts	National Reporter system, such as Pacific Reporter (675 P.2d 649 (Alaska App. 1983))	Same	Same		
State Trial Courts	Usually Unreported Occasionally an official reporter, such as Miscellaneous Reports* (N.Y.) (23 Misc. 2d 301 (Fam. Ct. 1980)) New York Supplement (222 N.Y.S. 2d 331 (Fam. Ct. 1980))	All decisions in General Digest System	Same		

*-denotes official reporter

The National Reporter System consists of

- seven **regional reporters:**
  - Atlantic
  - North Eastern
  - North Western
  - Pacific
  - South Eastern
  - Southern
  - South Western

- two special reporters for heavily populated states
  - *California Reporter*
  - *New York Supplement*

Each regional reporter contains decisions from a given geographical area of the country. For example, the *North Western Reporter* includes decisions from Iowa, Michigan, Minnesota, Nebraska, North and South Dakota, and Wisconsin.

While at one time it was thought that courts would be likely to follow the decisions of other courts in neighboring states, the grouping of states is today more a matter of tradition and convenience.

There are also a number of **specialized reporters** that gather court decisions in a particular branch of the law for easy reference. Examples include the *Federal Securities Law Reports*, the *Trade Regulation Reporter*, and the *Fair Employment Practices Cases*, to name a few. Unlike other reporters, which limit themselves to the decisions of specific courts but which include cases in all areas of the law, these specialized reporters publish cases from federal and state courts anywhere in the country. They are restricted to specific legal topics. For a legal practitioner who specializes heavily, they can be an invaluable resource.

Case reports are customarily issued in consecutively numbered bound volumes. Thus, for example, a case may appear at 389 U.S. 407: page 389 of volume 407 of the *United States Reports*.

Many reporters have more than one series. When the volumes of the first series reached a high number, the publisher started the numbering system over and called the new volumes a "second series." Thus, for example, there are nearly 1,000 volumes of the *Federal Reporter, Second Series*, containing cases dating back to 1925. West Publishing Company expects to begin a Third Series of the Federal Reporter in late 1993 or early 1994. In order to locate a particular case, therefore, it is important to know the series as well as the volume and page number.

A substantial amount of time elapses between the issuance of an opinion and its publication in a bound reporter volume. This delay is occasioned by the need for enough opinions to accumulate to fill a full volume, by the occasional need for correction of an opinion after it has been issued, and by the usual delays of publication. Where a rapidly-changing area of the law is involved, this delay can often cause problems for the legal researcher.

To eliminate these problems, various methods of getting opinions into the hands of those who need them prior to the publication of bound reporter volumes have been developed. Most reporters issue **advance sheets**, which are paperback versions of smaller groups of opinions that will eventually appear in the bound volumes. Whereas a bound volume may be issued from one to twenty times per year, advance sheets are often issued weekly, thus minimizing delay.

A few courts, such as the United States Supreme Court and the United States Court of Appeals for the Fifth Circuit, go one step further in streamlining the process. These courts issue **slip opinions**, individual decisions in booklet form, which are mailed directly to subscribers within days after the opinions are issued.

For the United States Supreme Court, decisions are likewise published rapidly in *United States Law Week*, a legal newsletter that also provides summaries of important decisions by other courts. A few state supreme courts have similar publications, such as the *Texas Supreme Court Journal*, which provides rapid publication of decisions of that court.

The primary source of legislative materials is the statutory code of the United States and of each state. These codes represent a collection of all general statutes, grouped by subject matter. Annual supplements, called **pocket parts** because they are fitted into a pocket in the back of each volume, keep the volumes up-to-date as the statutes are amended.

Many code volumes also contain **annotations** to court decisions interpreting the sections of the code that are contained in the volumes. Sometimes it is necessary to refer to a statute as it was when originally enacted or as of a specific time in the past. The session laws contain the text of statutes and statutory amendments precisely as they were enacted at a given session of the legislature. **Slip laws**, similar to slip opinions, are sometimes issued.

Federal legislative history is contained in the published committee hearings and reports of the Senate and the House of Representatives, together with the **Congressional Record**, which is a verbatim transcript of all proceedings on the floor of the Senate and House. Important committee reports are reprinted in *U.S. Code Congressional and Administrative News* published by West Publishing Company.

With occasional exceptions, usually for important statutes, no published materials are available on the legislative history of state statutes.

Administrative regulations are published in the *Code of Federal Regulations* and in similar volumes on the state level. Just as the session laws give the text of a statute as enacted, the Federal Register may be consulted to determine the text of a regulation at the time it was enacted. A few states have similar volumes.

Administrative rulings and decisions are published much as are judicial opinions. Some agencies have official reporters, such as the *Federal Trade Commission Decisions* and *National Transportation Safety Board Decisions*. These and other administrative decisions are also published in unofficial specialized reporters such as those described above.

Secondary sources abound, and the most that can be done here is to list the most commonly used materials. There are two principal legal encyclopedias in general use, entitled *American Jurisprudence (2d edition)*, nicknamed "AmJur," and *Corpus Juris Secundum*. Encyclopedias of state law are sometimes available.

Virtually every law school publishes at least one legal periodical (usually called a **law review** or **law journal**). Some major law schools publish several. A few legal periodicals, such as the *ABA Research Journal*, are not published by a law school.

Law reviews and journals feature articles on legal topics by noted legal scholars, including law professors and judges, together with material written by law students. While most law reviews are general in scope, a few are devoted to specific branches of the law (*e.g.*, the *Harvard Civil Rights - Civil Liberties Law Review*). Many law reviews place emphasis on the law of the state in which their sponsoring law schools are located.

Legal reference books, known as **treatises**, are often written by law professors and other legal scholars. These reference works, which may range from one thin volume to a twenty-volume set with periodic supplements, cover almost every conceivable legal topic. Their value, of course, depends upon the prestige and scholarly ability of the author.

An important set of legal reference works is the *Restatements of the Law*, published by the American Law Institute, which summarize the state of the law in a given area and indicate the trend of recent decisions.

Finally, **form books**, often written by practicing attorneys, provide sample forms of legal documents, such as wills, real estate documents, and court pleadings, that may be copied and adapted to fit a particular need.

As previously mentioned, some legal materials do not directly present the law but instead operate as aids to locating the law in other legal materials. First among these case-finding aids are **digests**. Each reported decision in the West Publishing Company reporter system is summarized in a series of **headnotes**, which are paragraphs written by the West editorial staff summarizing the important legal points contained in the decision. Each headnote is assigned to one or more topic designations that consist of the name of a legal topic (such as Negligence, Constitutional Law, and Federal Civil Procedure) and a number which represents a sub-topic within the general topic.

For each state, region, or other grouping, a **digest** is published that reprints these headnotes, grouping them in systematic fashion by topic and sub-topic. As new cases dealing with a given topic and sub-topic are decided, their headnotes appear, appropriately classified, in the pocket part of the appropriate digest volume. Thus, to find additional cases dealing with a particular topic and sub-topic, one need only consult the section of the appropriate digest dealing with that topic and sub-topic and then look up the cases that correspond to the headnotes listed under that topic and sub-topic.

Another important case-finding tool is *Shepard's Citations*. These volumes list, for each reported case, the later cases that have cited, or referred to, the case. Citing also includes noting information in a form that will permit the reader to locate the information and will give the important characteristics in a compact form.

Headnote numbers are also given. Thus, once one case has been found that is relevant to a particular topic, other cases on that point may be found by using *Shepard's* to determine what cases have cited the original case for the proposition being researched.

Computer-assisted legal research systems are an important case finding tool. Two such systems, LEXIS and WESTLAW, are now in widespread use. These databases contain the full text of both federal and state cases that have reached the appellate level over the past several decades. In addition, direct case histories (whether a case has been affirmed, reversed, granted certiorari, etc.) are available at the federal level as far back as pre-revolutionary days, and at the state level back to the late nineteenth century.

Cases available in full text may be searched for a given word or combination of words relevant to the research topic, such as a subject, issue, name (i.e. party, judge, witness, etc.), or any other important reference. Once cases have been located, the researcher can examine the case synopsis, headnotes or the entire text, either on screen or by printing a case for future reference. In addition, sophisticated citation capabilities allow a researcher to Shepardize, as well as locate and verify parallel citations.

Techniques of Legal Research.

There is no one correct way to locate materials on a legal topic. For example, where the research question involves federal taxation, an appropriate starting point might be the Internal Revenue Code. With a question on the law of negligence, the researcher might turn to the *Restatement (Second) of Torts*, a treatise or law review article on torts, a legal encyclopedia, or a digest topic under the heading of "Torts" or "Negligence."

While the starting point depends on the nature of the problem, common starting places include digest topics, annotations to statutes, legal encyclopedias, the *Index to Legal Periodicals*, the index to *American Law Reports* (a collection of selected cases and articles relating to the cases), and treatises.

Another approach is to use a computerized research system. LEXIS and WESTLAW provide the legal researcher with literally thousands of databases containing not only cases, but federal annotated statutes, state annotated statutes, Restatements, administrative law, regulations, federal tax abstracts, law review articles, law dictionary and encyclopedia entries and much more. In addition, through NEXIS and DIALOG, these services give the researcher access to the text of newspapers, magazines, journals, abstracts, lists, and other data often critical to the outcome of a legal matter. For example, similar matters that are settled out of court or that have not yet reached the appellate level are often reported in newspapers and professional journals. Another common use of these ancillary databases is the location and verification of expert witnesses, including educational credentials, professional writings, and even challenges from other professionals to an expert's opinions and points of view.

With many research problems, the starting point may be the ending point as well. Where only a quick answer to a simple problem is sought, it may not be necessary to refer to a wide variety of materials to research every aspect of a particular branch of law. For example, if what is needed is the statute of limitations for burglary, it will seldom be useful to locate the appropriate statute in the appropriate jurisdiction and then to look up all cases decided under that statute, read all the law review articles ever written about burglary, compare the statutes of the other 49 states, and write a 20-page memorandum on the subject. In such a situation, an answer such as "four years" may be all that is necessary.

In more complicated research projects, the first materials that the researcher consults seldom provide all the information that is needed. The materials may not answer the precise question under investigation but instead answer a different, although related, question.

Alternatively, the legal question may be the same but the facts of the case that has been found differ somewhat from the facts of the case under investigation. Even if the facts and the law are the same, the researcher may want to investigate further to be sure that the legal principle has not been changed or that exceptions to it have not been created.

Finally, even where the material answers the question (is "on point," in legal research parlance), it may be helpful to have more cases or other materials that state the same legal principle, for added persuasive value in convincing a court to adopt a particular position. This is especially true where the case on point is from a different jurisdiction or from a lower court and a similar case from the correct jurisdiction or from a higher court is sought.

Obtaining further materials once the first materials have been located is usually not difficult, since each set of materials contains clues suggesting the avenues that the researcher should explore next. Statute books usually contain case annotations; cases and other materials contain citations to relevant legal materials. "Bridges," such as the digest system and *Shepard's Citations*, can be used to find further materials.

Where the researcher is dealing primarily with judicial opinions, all relevant cases can be located in a systematic way once the first case has been found. Cases decided before the first case may be found by checking the digest topics under which the headnotes of the original case are classified or by looking up the cases that the original case cites in support of the relevant proposition.

Cases decided after this first case may be found by using the digest or by "**Shepardizing**" the original case to locate later cases that have cited it.

Finally, the later history of the first case itself may be determined from *Shepard's Citations*. If the case has been affirmed or reversed on appeal, this will materially affect the answer to the question being researched. Both LEXIS and WESTLAW provide researchers with the ability to Shepardize and track headnotes via computer, which saves time and increases accuracy.

Where does it all stop? Cases lead to more cases, which lead to more cases, and so on -- if the researcher is lucky. In such a situation, research should continue until the precise question is answered by the highest authority in the controlling jurisdiction, or until the researcher determines that he or she has come as close to the exact answer as is reasonably possible.

The approach depends on the circumstances. It may be that only a "quick look" for an approximate and probably correct answer being all that is needed. Or, the researcher may be preparing a Supreme Court brief or law review article in which every fine point must be meticulously tracked down.

A frequent occurrence, especially where the question is detailed or abstract or where the branch of law being researched is new, is that too few materials are located. Either no "first case" or other material can be found, or the line of cases is too short or never answers the precise question. In such a situation, a new approach, trying legal materials not consulted on the first attempt, may open up a promising line of cases. Alternatively, the question itself must be reformulated, and materials on analogous points must be sought. In such a situation, it will often be necessary to consult with the person requesting the research.

Finally, the inability to find relevant materials does not necessarily signify failure. There are many legal questions that have never been addressed by the law. Knowing that this is the case may be as valuable as finding the exact answer would have been.

For an excellent and more detailed discussion of the basics of legal research, see M. Cohen, *Legal Research in a Nutshell.* Detailed rules for citing legal materials may be found in *A Uniform System of Citations*, often known as the "blue book," published by leading law reviews.

TERMS TO KNOW

legal research
citation
stare decisis
precedent
statutes
common law
legislative history
secondary sources
reporters
official reports
unofficial reporters
specialized reporters
advance sheets
slip opinions
pocket parts
annotation
slip laws
Congressional Record
law review
law journal
treatises
form books
digest
headnotes
computer assisted legal research
Shepardizing

FOOTNOTES

1. 28 U.S.C. §120.
2. 15 U.S.C. §1.

CHAPTER VI

FEDERAL COURTS

In recent years, the federal courts have exerted an ever-increasing influence over virtually every aspect of American life. In addition to adjudicating ordinary damage disputes between private litigants, federal courts have become involved in social issues ranging from school desegregation and prison reform to abortion and the death penalty. Yet few Americans have a good understanding of the inner workings of the federal courts or the sources of and limitations on their authority. Since virtually every legal professional inevitably comes into contact with the federal courts at some time or other, a working understanding of their powers and procedures is essential.

Jurisdiction.

1. Cases the Federal Courts May Hear.

Under the Constitution, the federal courts are courts of **limited jurisdiction** that can only hear those types of cases the Constitution empowers them to hear. All other sorts of cases not explicitly or implicitly set forth in the Constitution's grant of jurisdiction can only be heard in state courts.

The two most significant jurisdictional grants included in the Constitution are, first, jurisdiction over all cases arising under the Constitution, laws, and treaties of the United States, or **federal question jurisdiction**, and, second, cases involving disputes between parties from different states, or **diversity jurisdiction**.

2. Federal Question Jurisdiction.

The language of the Constitution, giving federal courts jurisdiction over all cases involving disputes "arising under" the Constitution, laws, and treaties of the United States, has no clear and precise definition. In fact, none of the various definitions that the courts have given to the term "arising under" seems to encompass all the different cases. Perhaps the best definition is that of a "substantial claim founded 'directly' upon federal law."[1] Even this definition is not easy to understand -- what is direct and what is indirect? In fact, although the term is difficult to define, courts and litigants alike seem to understand it reasonably well in practice. Some examples of federal question cases are disputes involving the federal income tax laws, the federal securities laws, the federal bankruptcy laws, or claims that constitutional rights have been violated.

3. Diversity Of Citizenship.

Cases that involve disputes between citizens of different states, or between a state government and a citizen of another state, or between a citizen of a state and foreign government or foreign individual, are referred to as **diversity of citizenship** actions. When there is genuine diversity of citizenship and where more than $50,000 is in controversy, the federal District Court has jurisdiction. The basic examples of diversity of citizenship jurisdiction are:

a. Disputes between citizens of different states. Example.: A citizen of New York sues a citizen of New Jersey.

b. Disputes between citizens of a state and a citizen of a foreign state. Example: A citizen of California sues a citizen of the People's Republic of China.

c. Disputes between citizens of one state and a foreign state. Example: A citizen of California sues the People's Republic of China.

d. Disputes between citizens of different states and a foreign state. Example: Citizens of California and Oregon sue the People's Republic of China.

e. Disputes between two or more states. Example: Texas and Oklahoma sue New Mexico.

f. Disputes between a citizen of one state and the government of another state. Example: a citizen of New York sues Massachusetts. (However, many such suits are barred by the Eleventh Amendment.)

The historical reason for granting federal District Courts diversity of citizenship jurisdiction was the fear that the state courts in which these cases might be tried would be biased against non-citizens. In order to avoid any hint of bias or prejudice, a neutral forum for diversity of citizenship cases is provided in the federal courts.

4. Exclusive Jurisdiction.

The Constitution contains a number of very specific grants of jurisdiction that have been construed to be "exclusive." A case over which the federal courts have **exclusive jurisdiction** is one that the state courts have no authority to hear. Among those very narrow grants of exclusive jurisdiction are:

- all cases of admiralty or maritime jurisdiction
- all cases affecting ambassadors and other public ministers and consuls
- all cases in which the United States is a party.

There are many other sorts of cases over which the federal courts have exclusive jurisdiction that are not explicitly set forth in the Constitution, but instead are "federal question" cases. The following are a few examples:

- bankruptcy proceedings
- cases arising under the patent or copyright laws
- cases involving customs
- cases involving some sort of penalty under a federal law
- cases involving interstate commerce and antitrust actions.

5. Criminal Jurisdiction.

As a part of their "federal question" jurisdiction, the United States District courts have a broad jurisdiction over all offenses that are against the laws of the United States. This jurisdiction, as defined by statute, is exclusive.[2]

The Supreme Court has ruled that there are no federal "common law crimes."[3] In other words, a federal crime must clearly be defined by an act of Congress. The United States Code, the body of law in which most federal statutes are recorded, enumerates a broad variety of federal crimes.[4]

It is possible that an act might violate both a federal and state law and thus constitute both a federal and a state crime. The offender may then be prosecuted by either the federal or the state court or both without violating the rule against placing a person in **double jeopardy**.

6. Pendent Jurisdiction.

Pendent jurisdiction allows the federal District Court to make decisions on matters that would otherwise be exclusively in the jurisdiction of a state court. If a federal court already has jurisdiction over a case, it may extend its jurisdiction to other matters raised in that case, even though the court otherwise would not have jurisdiction over those matters had they been presented independently.

For example, a plaintiff might bring suit claiming injury as a result of the defendant's violation of certain federal securities laws. Such a case raises a "federal question" and is properly within the jurisdiction of the federal court. That same plaintiff might claim that the defendant committed common law fraud. The common law fraud claim is normally a state claim over which the federal court has no jurisdiction. Because the plaintiff raised it in the federal case, however, the federal court has the power to hear it. This rule avoids wasteful and duplicitous litigation that would result if the plaintiff had to file a separate suit in state court to have his or her common law fraud claim adjudicated.

Judicial Restraint.

The courts within the federal system are constantly struggling with the problem of how to sift through the thousands of cases filed each year and determine which ones present the type of controversy that they should hear. Both the trial courts and the appellate courts in the federal system have adopted certain criteria to resolve this problem. Collectively this set of criteria is known as the **doctrine of judicial self-restraint**.

Judicial self-restraint is the practice of using these criteria to refuse to accept jurisdiction in certain cases. If the federal courts did not exercise some sort of restraint, they would quickly be submerged under a steadily increasing tide of incoming cases. Some of the more important principles of judicial restraint[5] are:

1. Justiciable Controversy.

The Constitution requires that before the federal courts accept jurisdiction over a matter, a "case or controversy" must exist. Courts have interpreted this Constitutional directive to mean that a case:

- must be between *bona fide* adversaries, *and*
- must involve
  - the protection or enforcement of valuable legal rights, *or*
  - the punishment, prevention, or redress of wrongs that directly concern the party or parties bringing suit.

The matter must be definite, and the remedy requested must be capable of being granted through specific relief such as a specific amount of damages or an injunction. Should two friends try to use the courts to decide whose home is more aesthetically appealing, to decide whose child is a better baseball player, or simply to settle a friendly wager, no **justiciable controversy** would be presented. The parties would not actually be adversaries. They would not be asking the court to grant any specific relief but would instead be asking it to make a value judgment.

2. Standing.

A person bringing suit must have a personal stake in the litigation of a sufficient nature to justify the federal court in accepting jurisdiction. **Standing**, as this personal stake is usually called, is measured by determining whether the litigant can establish a sufficient personal economic interest in the controversy or whether the litigant claims that his or her own basic rights are being violated.

A person residing in Palo Alto, California, who owns no real property within the limits of the City of San Francisco would not have standing to sue the Corps of Engineers, a federal agency, in federal court to obtain an injunction to prevent the Corps from building a dam that would flood residential property in San Francisco. Not being a resident or property owner, the Palo Alto resident would have no economic interest at stake. Actual property owners whose property would be affected would have standing to sue in federal court.

3. Advisory Opinions.

The federal courts will not issue "advisory opinions." **Advisory opinions** are judicial rulings upon the legality of governmental actions, whether already accomplished or contemplated, when there is no *bona fide* case or controversy to decide. The rule against advisory opinions was first established when the Supreme Court refused to answer twenty-nine questions proposed by Secretary of State Thomas Jefferson in 1793.[6]

Because of the rule against advisory opinions, the Congress, in deciding whether to enact a particular law, cannot ask the Supreme Court for its opinion as to whether, if passed, the law would be unconstitutional. Instead, the Supreme Court may only address the question of the law's constitutionality after Congress has enacted the law and a person who claims that the law violates his or her constitutional rights has brought suit in federal court.

4. Political Questions.

Federal courts have also refused to decide "political questions" in cases involving certain legislative or executive actions. In declining jurisdiction over such matters, courts have relied on the policies of separation of powers and judicial self-restraint.[7] The principal application of this doctrine is to questions of international and domestic law that immediately concern the country's political or military interaction with foreign nations.[8]

Other examples of political questions are cases involving the processes by which statutes or constitutional amendments are adopted[9] and questions about which group is the legitimate government of a particular state.[10]

5. Hypothetical Questions.

A hypothetical question involving an intellectual difference of opinion, as opposed to a real dispute, will not be entertained by the federal courts.[11] Such great philosophical debates as the existence of God or the presence of life on other planets are too vague and imprecise to present the concrete issues necessary to litigate in court. One federal District Court judge refused to accept jurisdiction in a case where a man sued God because the United States Marshals were unable to serve a summons on the defendant.[12]

6. Mootness.

A moot case is one that does not present a case or controversy because the matter has already been resolved. Something has happened to the case before the court has decided it, rendering any action by the court unnecessary. Suppose, for instance, that a city passes an ordinance making it illegal for a woman to be a firefighter. A woman who wants to become a firefighter files a lawsuit in federal District Court seeking to have the ordinance declared unconstitutional and to have the city enjoined from enforcing it. Before the case is filed or before it comes to trial, the city repeals the ordinance, passes a resolution pledging that it will never enact a similar ordinance and hires the plaintiff as a firefighter with back pay. Here the matter has been resolved. It is moot, and nothing remains for the court to decide.

Structure of the Federal Courts.

Article III of the Constitution creates the Supreme Court and empowers the Congress to create such other lower federal courts as it deems necessary. Congress has used this constitutional grant of power to establish two levels of courts below the Supreme Court. At the lowest level are the United States District Courts, which are the trial courts of the federal system. The middle level is the United States Courts of Appeals.

Let us now examine the complementary roles of these three tiers: the District Courts, the Courts of Appeals and the Supreme Court.

1. Federal District Courts.

More than six hundred federal district judges preside over the 94 judicial districts that cover the United States and its territories. Naturally, the more sparsely populated judicial districts have fewer judges than the heavily populated districts. In fact, in the least populated areas some federal district judges may serve several districts. Some heavily populated judicial districts, on the other hand, may contain as many as twenty-eight judges. Congress establishes the district configuration, basing it on such factors as population, distance, and case-load.[13]

Federal district court judges are required to reside in the district in which they sit. Their offices are maintained in a principal city in the district, usually at the nearest federal office building.

Each District has a number of federal officers and agencies that assist the federal district Courts in the administration of justice, including a United States District Clerk's Office, a United States Marshal's Office and a United States Attorney's Office. These supporting officers and agencies are discussed in detail later in this chapter.

With limited exceptions discussed in the section on the Supreme Court, these district courts conduct the trials of all cases in the federal judicial system. In these cases, the district court judge supervises pre-trial matters, conducts the trial, and enters the judgment.

The district judge may decide to write an opinion on the issues of law or fact in a particular case. Such opinions often are published to provide guidance for other courts faced with similar issues. They appear in the *Federal Supplement.*

As a court of record, the district court has a court reporter or an electronic recording device present at all times to transcribe proceedings. If one of the litigants later decides to appeal the decision of the district judge, the appellate court may refer to this complete record of the district court proceedings.

2. United States Courts of Appeals.

The United States Courts of Appeals are the intermediate appellate courts in the federal judicial system. The main purpose of these courts is to hear appeals from district court decisions, thereby facilitating the prompt disposition of cases and easing the caseload of the Supreme Court.

There are thirteen United States Courts of Appeals, one in each of twelve geographic regions known as circuits, plus a thirteenth court -- the United States Court of Appeals for the Federal Circuit -- that hears appeals in certain patent, copyright, and other special cases.

Each circuit, with the exception of the District of Columbia Circuit, encompasses three or more states or territories. The Ninth Circuit is the largest in area, embracing nine states and the territory of Guam. A Court of Appeals has a city in which it usually sits, but it may also sit in other cities in the states it serves. Each Court of Appeals has jurisdiction to hear appeals from federal courts and administrative agencies operating within its circuit.

Currently there are some 200 judges serving on these courts in the thirteen circuits, with eleven new appellate court positions added by Congress under the Omnibus Judgeship Act of 1990. Each court is composed of at least four judges with the largest court, the Ninth Circuit, now having twenty-eight judges. The Chief Judge of a particular circuit is the judge with the longest active service who has not yet reached his or her 70th birthday.

Most cases appealed to the Courts of Appeals are heard by panels of not more than three judges.[14] When a case is heard by a panel, there must be at least two judges present, and at least two must agree before there is a valid decision.[15]

Sometimes, however, all the judges in a particular circuit sit ***en banc*** to hear a case. When a hearing *en banc* is ordered by a majority of the judges in regular active service on a United States Court of Appeals, then all the active judges on the court sit to determine the result in the case.[16] A majority of the active judges in the circuit sitting *en banc* constitutes a quorum, and a majority has the authority to render a decision.

En banc courts are the exception rather than the rule. Only in cases of great importance to the circuit as a whole, and possibly to the nation, do all the judges of a federal court of appeals sit *en banc* to determine major developments in the law.[17]

The primary advantages of *en banc* decisions are avoiding conflicts of views and promoting finality among the judges within a particular circuit.[18] Their major disadvantages, especially since the number of judgeships in each circuit has been expanded, are the difficulties in convening all the judges in the circuit and the enormous length of time it sometimes takes to render a decision.

The United States courts of appeals are primarily appellate courts that hear appeals from final decisions of United States district courts.[19] A **final decision** has been defined as one that ends the litigation on the merits and leaves nothing for the court to do but to execute the judgment.[20]

There are certain cases, however, in which an appeal may be pursued even though the judgment of the district court is **interlocutory**, not final. Interlocutory orders are rulings of the court that do not finally dispose of the case but require some further action of the court before a final decision can be rendered. Appeal may be had from an interlocutory order by a federal district judge to the United States courts of appeals in the following circumstances:[21]

a. Interlocutory orders dealing with injunctions, except where direct review may be had in the Supreme Court.

b. Interlocutory orders appointing receivers or affecting receivers. (A **receiver** is a neutral party who is appointed by a court to preserve property during the course of the litigation).

c. Interlocutory decrees determining the rights and liabilities of parties to admiralty cases.

d. Certain bankruptcy decisions.[22]

In addition to hearing the appeals of criminal and civil cases decided by the federal district courts, the United States courts of appeals hear most appeals from orders of federal administrative agencies.[23] The tax court is considered an administrative agency for appellate purposes, and the court of appeals is the proper forum to review its decisions.[24]

Under the Federal Rules of Civil Procedure, the procedure for filing an appeal to the court of appeals is simple. First, a litigant must file a notice of appeal, which is an uncomplicated document. Defects in the notice of appeal that are not material can be waived so long as the appellee is not mislead by the defect and the intention to appeal clearly appears. In civil cases, notice of appeal must be filed within thirty days after the entry of the judgment except when the United States is appealing, in which case sixty days are allowed. Notice of appeal must be filed within ten days in criminal cases.

An appellant must also file the record on appeal, must docket the appeal, and must file both his or her brief and the appendix. Each court of appeals appoints a clerk who makes sure that all these documents are properly and timely filed.

Decisions of the United States courts of appeals are required to be in writing, stating facts and making conclusions of law. The courts of appeals have a duty to follow majority opinions of the Supreme Court[25] just as United States district courts are bound by the law established by the appeals court in the circuit in which they are located.[26] All decisions of the courts of appeals are reported in the *Federal Reporter* series published by West Publishing Company.

3. United States Supreme Court.

At the pinnacle of the federal judicial system sits the Supreme Court of the United States. The first legislative act to define its jurisdiction was the Judiciary Act of 1789, which made it clear that the individual states, Congress, and the President were subject to the Court's judicial authority.[27] The Judiciary Act required members of the Court to travel twice a year to distant parts of the nation and preside over courts of appeals sitting in various circuits, a practice that soon fell into disfavor with the Justices.[28]

The Supreme Court was created as a poor relation during its first century and a half, shuffled from New York to Philadelphia to a vacant part of the U.S. Senate in Washington. It was not until 1935 that the Supreme Court obtained a home of its own -- the present extraordinary and overwhelming Supreme Court Building designed by architect Cass Gilbert.[29]

Like other federal judges, the Chief Justice and the eight Associate Justices are appointed by the President with the advice and consent of the Senate and serve for life. The presence of six Justices constitutes a quorum, and five Justices must agree before a decision of the Supreme Court becomes official and binding.[30] The regular term of the Supreme Court always commences on the first Monday in October of each year and continues until the latter part of June.[31] On rare occasions, the Court will convene in special session during the summer to hear important cases, such as the Nixon tapes case and President Truman's seizure of the steel mills.

The Chief Justice of the United States, in addition to the primary function of presiding over the sessions and deliberations of the Court, has many important administrative functions that often take him far from the chambers of that august body. The Constitution requires the Chief Justice to preside over impeachment trials of the President in the Senate, a duty that the Chief Justice has only had to exercise once during the history of our nation.

By statute, the Chief Justice is chair of both the Federal Judicial Center and the Judicial Conference of the United States. The Federal Judicial Center is the research and development arm of the federal judiciary and plays an important role in the training of new federal judges. Acting as a kind of board of directors for the more than 600 federal judges, the Judicial Conference of the United States considers such problems as proposed legislation in new areas of law, the need for increased efficiency of court calendars, and more efficient use of jurors' time. Former Chief Justice Warren Burger estimated that nearly a third of his time is spent on administrative and cultural duties that have little to do with the juridic functions of the Court.

The Supreme Court exercises both a limited original jurisdiction and an extensive appellate jurisdiction. Jurisdiction of the Supreme Court extends to criminal and to civil matters. The Court's jurisdiction may be **exclusive**, *i.e.*, the Court may be the only forum where a particular type of case can be tried, or it may be **non-exclusive**, *i.e.*, the Court may share its jurisdiction with other federal and/or state courts.

The Court's jurisdiction is complex and often confusing.

a. Direct Review of the Decisions of Federal District Courts.

There are four circumstances when an appeal may be made from a federal district court directly to the Supreme Court without first going through the United States court of appeals.

▸ Any civil action brought by the United States seeking to

- obtain equitable relief for violation of the antitrust laws

- enforce provisions of the Interstate Commerce Act, or

- recover under the common carriers section of the Communications Act where the district court judge makes an order stating that immediate consideration of the appeal by the Supreme Court is of such general public importance that it requires the Court's attention due to its significance in the administration of justice.[32]

- Appeals from an order granting or denying an interlocutory or permanent injunction in any civil action that is required to be heard by a three-judge federal district court.[33] (In 1976, Congress drastically limited the circumstances under which a three-judge federal district court may be convened.)

- Appeals from an interlocutory or final judgment of any federal court holding an Act of Congress unconstitutional in any civil action, suit or proceeding to which the United States, or any of its agencies, officers or employees are a party.[34]

b. Review of Decisions of the Courts of Appeals.

There are two basic circumstances under which cases are appealed from the United States courts of appeals to the Supreme Court:

- Review by **writ of certiorari** upon the petition of any party to the suit in the court of appeals.[35] This is the most commonly used means of appeal from circuit court decisions. The Supreme Court has the discretion to decide which applications for writ of certiorari it will grant. The court frequently "grants cert" to resolve conflicts between circuit court decisions or to decide new and significant issues of law.

- Review by appeal from a court of appeals where:

  - The appellate court has held an Act of Congress unconstitutional in a case to which the United States is a party.[36]

  - A court of appeals has held a state statute unconstitutional or in conflict with the laws and treaties of the United States.[37]

There is a third, rarely-used method of taking appeals from the United States courts of appeals to the Supreme Court. This method is by **certificate**. A federal court of appeals may issue a certification to the Supreme Court asking for instructions in either a criminal or civil case.[38] Certificates are issued only for questions of law, and these questions must be distinct and definite.[39]

c. Review of State Court Decisions - Direct Review.

The Supreme Court may also review a decision from the highest court of a state when:[40]

- The highest court in the state has rendered a final judgment;

and when:

- the validity of a treaty or statute of the United States is drawn into question; or

- the validity of a state statute is drawn into question on the basis of its conflicting with the Constitution, treaties or laws of the United States; or

- any title, right, privilege, or immunity is specifically claimed under the Constitution, under treaties or statutes of the United States, or under a commission held or authorized or exercised by or under the authority of the United States. The Supreme Court's power to review cases under this provision does not depend on the amount in controversy or on diversity of citizenship, but upon the existence of a genuine federal question.[41]

d. Original Jurisdiction.

The Constitution states that "in all Cases affecting Ambassadors, other public ministers and consuls, and those in which a State shall be a party, the Supreme Court shall have original jurisdiction."[42]

Original jurisdiction means jurisdiction to hear and decide a case at its inception as a trial court would, rather than hearing it on appeal. Therefore, this constitutional provision means that in certain types of cases, the Supreme Court may function as a trial court and decide all issues of law and fact.

The Supreme Court's original jurisdiction is of two types: exclusive and non-exclusive. Those cases over which it exercises both original and exclusive jurisdiction may only originate and be tried in the Supreme Court. As to other cases over which its original jurisdiction is non-exclusive, the Supreme Court shares its original jurisdiction concurrently with the lower federal courts. Parties may bring such cases either in the Supreme Court or in a federal district court.

The Supreme Court has original and exclusive jurisdiction in the following types of cases:[43]

- Suits instituted by one state against another state. *Example*: The State of Texas sues the State of Oklahoma over the correct boundary of the Red River.

- Suits, actions, or proceedings against ambassadors or other public ministers of foreign states or their domestics or domestic servants, not inconsistent with the law of nations. *Example*: A California bank sues the ambassador of Canada for breach of contract. Note that fewer than three cases have been considered under this clause in the entire history of the Court.[44]

- A suit by a state against citizens of another country. *Example*: The State of New York sues an Iranian student to deport the student. This type of jurisdiction, although not granted by Congress, has been held to be within the province of the Supreme Court.[45]

The Supreme Court has original but non-exclusive jurisdiction in the following types of cases:

- Suits by the United States against a state. *Example*: The United States sues the State of New York to recover federal grant funds that have been spent improperly.

- Suits by a state against a foreign country. *Example*: Texas sues Mexico to establish the boundaries of the Rio Grande River. (Here again, the Court's jurisdiction is based on constitutional and not statutory provisions.)[46]

- Suits by a state against citizens of another state or against aliens. *Example*: The State of Missouri sues a citizen of the State of Oklahoma for failure to obtain a proper license for the Oklahoman's business in Missouri. Since this jurisdiction is not exclusive, this type of case could be brought in the federal district court or in state court.

- Actions and proceedings brought by ambassadors or other public ministers of foreign states or to which consuls or vice consuls of foreign states are parties. *Example*: The Canadian ambassador sues a local auto repair shop for damages for defective workmanship on his embassy automobile.

Despite this grant of original jurisdiction, full-blown trials with the parade of witnesses, objections, and arguments of attorneys and the presentation of evidence that we would normally associate with a trial on the merits in federal district court rarely occur.

Although a federal statute grants parties the right of a trial by jury in original actions in the Supreme Court against citizens of the United States,[47] no jury trial has been held in the Court since the 18th century.[48] Instead, the Supreme Court typically appoints a distinguished lawyer or retired judge to serve as master and to hear the evidence and make recommendations to the Court.

Procedure.

Procedure in the federal district courts is governed by the Federal Rules of Civil Procedure. These rules tell the parties how to:

- file a lawsuit
- pursue pre-trial preparation
- conduct themselves during a trial, and
- obtain a final binding judgment.

Although these rules and the underlying federal procedural system vary from those in the different state courts, they are remarkably similar to state systems in many ways. This similarity results in part from the fact that many state systems have modified their rules to be more in line with the federal system. Thus, a student who studies federal procedure also inevitably learns principles that are applicable to the various state systems.

1. The Complaint.

An action commences in federal court with the filing of a **complaint** with the court pursuant to Rule 3. Pursuant to Rule 8, this complaint must contain three essential elements:

- A "short and plain statement of the claim showing that the pleader is entitled to relief;"
- A statement of the ground on which the court's jurisdiction is based;
- A demand for judgment for the relief that the plaintiff seeks.

"A short and plain statement of the claim" has generally been construed to require a simple statement of circumstances demonstrating that the plaintiff has been wronged.

A complaint's purpose is to inform the defendant and the court of the basis of the plaintiff's claim -- nothing more. The defendant is entitled to find out all the details in the process described below known as **discovery**.

2. The Defendant's Response to the Complaint.

When a defendant has been served with a complaint, the Federal Rules require that the defendant make a response. Just as the plaintiff must let the defendant know the grounds of the plaintiff's claim, the defendant must reveal his or her defenses. The defendant may assert numerous defenses, such as:

- that the claim cannot be brought in any federal court because those courts lack jurisdiction;
- that the claim cannot be brought in that particular federal court, either because that court does not have jurisdiction over the defendant or because the federal venue rules require that under the circumstances the case should be brought in a different federal court;
- that a necessary party to the lawsuit has not been joined.

These defenses have nothing to do with the merits of the plaintiff's claim. There are, however, other defenses that do address the merits:

- that the plaintiff's claim is untrue - this is a **denial**;

- that the law does not entitle the plaintiff to relief based on the facts alleged;

- that even if what the plaintiff claims is true, the defendant has an **affirmative defense**; that is, that other pertinent facts relieve the defendant of liability. *Example*: Whether or not the defendant may have been responsible for the plaintiff's injuries, the plaintiff has waited too long to sue and the **statute of limitations** has run out.

Finally, while it is true that the plaintiff's complaint need only contain a "short and plain statement," Federal Rule 12(e) states that it cannot be "so vague and ambiguous that a party cannot reasonably be expected to interpose his responsive pleadings." The defendant may object to the complaint on such grounds and request that the plaintiff be required to file a more definite statement.

The next question is: how may the defendant present these various defenses and obligations? The Federal Rules provide two means.

First, all matters may be raised in an **answer**. Second, certain enumerated defenses set forth in Rule 12(b) may, at the option of the defendant, be raised by **motion**. These defenses are:

- lack of jurisdiction over the person
- lack of jurisdiction over the subject matter
- improper venue
- insufficiency of process
- insufficiency of service of process

- failure to state a claim on which relief can be granted
- failure to join a necessary party.

In Rule 7(b)(1) a **motion** is defined as "an application to the court for an order." In other words, it is a document in which a party requests the court to take certain action.

The various motions that defendants may file to assert any of the seven defenses set forth above are collectively known as **motions to dismiss**. If the court denies the defendant's motion to dismiss, or if the defendant chooses not to file such a motion, then the defendant must file an answer.

3. Counterclaims.

Often controversies arise in which each party claims to have been wronged by the other. After one party sues the other, the defendant wants to assert his or her own claim against the plaintiff. This may be a claim growing out of the same set of facts on which the plaintiff's claim is based, or it might be based on an entirely different incident. Rather than requiring the defendant to file a separate lawsuit, the Federal Rules permit the defendant to file a **counterclaim** against the plaintiff in the same action.

There are two types of counterclaims: **compulsory** and **permissive**. A compulsory counterclaim is one arising out of the same transaction or occurrence that is the subject matter of the plaintiff's action. Failure to assert a compulsory counterclaim in the defendant's answer bars the defendant from raising that claim in the future, either in the pending action or in the defendant's own separate lawsuit against the plaintiff.

A permissive counterclaim is a claim that the defendant has against the plaintiff that arises out of a separate incident. For example, the plaintiff claims that the defendant negligently drove into the plaintiff's car; the defendant claims that the plaintiff breached a contract with the defendant.

Under Rule 13(b), the defendant may assert his or her counterclaim against the plaintiff, but the defendant is not required to do so. If the defendant chooses not to raise it, he or she may later bring an action against the plaintiff.

4. Discovery.

After the parties have completed the pleading process described above, each side may only have a very sketchy view of its adversary's position. If the parties had no other means of finding out what their opponents could prove, they would be faced with countless surprises at trial against which they might be ill-equipped to defend. For example, one side might introduce unexpected testimony that the opposing side could have effectively rebutted had it only known in advance.

To avoid these problems, the Federal Rules provide for "discovery." Through use of the discovery tools created by the Rules, a party can become thoroughly acquainted with an adversary's position and with the testimony of the opponent's witnesses. A party has the opportunity to prepare his or her best possible case and to dispose of non-existent issues.

Often, discovery encourages **settlement**. Each party learns the strengths and weaknesses of his or her own and the opponent's positions and is better able to assess likelihood of success and, hence, the monetary value of the case.

Rule 26 prescribes the scope of discovery. The rule states that the parties "may obtain discovery regarding any matter, not privileged, which is relevant to the subject matter involved in the pending action." This includes, among other things:

- the identity and location of persons
- their knowledge of the subject matter
- the existence, location, and content of relevant documents.

Rule 26 adds that discovery may be had even if "the information sought will be inadmissible at trial, if the information sought appears to be reasonably calculated to lead to the discovery of admissible evidence."

The following are the various means of discovery:

a. Deposition upon oral examination

A **deposition** is the oral examination by any party of any person whom the party believes has relevant information. The taking of deposition testimony is like the taking of trial testimony. The entire process is recorded by a court reporter.

First, the deponent is sworn by the court reporter, who is a Notary Public. Then the party taking the deposition questions the deponent in the same format that is used at trial. The opposing party may make objections to the questions or answers.

When a party objects to a question, one of several things may happen. If the party objects on the ground that the question inquires into matters that are within the scope of discovery but inadmissible at trial, the court reporter merely records the objection and the deposition proceeds. Then, if the deposing party later wants to introduce the deposition at trial, the judge will rule on the validity of the objection, and, depending on the judge's ruling, either admit or exclude the testimony. In order to speed up the deposition, attorneys taking depositions often agree (**stipulate**) that this type of objection may be made at the time of trial.

If the party objects to the question because it is not within the scope of discovery, his or her opponent may simply withdraw the question. Sometimes, the objecting party instead may decide to let the inquiry proceed. Occasionally, however, the objecting party will instruct the witness not to answer the question. In that case, the party taking the deposition may decide to file with the court a **motion to compel**. Such motion asks the judge to rule that the witness must answer.

b. Interrogatories.

Another commonly used method of discovery is the use of **interrogatories**. Interrogatories are a series of written questions that one party submits to another that must be answered in writing and under oath. Interrogatories, like questions in a deposition, may relate to any matter not privileged that is relevant to the subject matter of the pending action.

The party on whom the interrogatories are served may object to any or all interrogatories on various grounds. Some examples of common objections are that an interrogatory inquires into matters that are privileged or beyond the scope of discovery or that it is overly burdensome.

Interrogatories are frequently used to gather preliminary information about the opponent's position and about any expert witnesses that a party intends to call at trial. An interrogatory may inquire about the subject matter of the expert's planned testimony and the grounds of the expert's opinions.

Interrogatories have the advantage of being comparatively simple and inexpensive. They do not provide the examining party with the flexibility of a deposition, however, in which the questioner may ask follow-up questions and probe the witnesses' responses in depth. Moreover, interrogatories, unlike depositions, may only be directed to parties in the case and not to third persons.

c. Requests for Admissions.

Another useful discovery device is the **Request for Admissions**. One party may send to the other written requests that the recipient admit or deny the truth of any matter within the scope of discovery that relates to statements or opinions of fact or to the application of law to fact, including the genuineness of any document described in the request.

The Federal Rules state that if the opponent fails to answer any request for admission within thirty days, the unanswered request is deemed admitted. The opponent, instead of answering a request, may object to it on various grounds including, but not limited to,

- that the request requires the revelation of privileged material

- that the request inquires into matters that are beyond the scope of discovery

- that the request is argumentative, ambiguous and unclear.

If the opponent does not object to the request, he or she must either admit or deny, or state in detail why he or she cannot admit or deny the matter.

Often a party will be unable to respond to a request for admission because he or she lacks the requisite information or knowledge. The Federal Rules specifically state that lack of information or knowledge is a permissible reason not to admit or deny the truth of the request. Requests for admissions are useful devices for discovering the areas of agreement between the parties and sharpening the focus of disputed matters.

d. Production of Documents.

Federal Rule 34 provides that a party may serve on any other party a **request to produce**, and to permit the party making the request to inspect and copy, any designated documents. A party may also request the opportunity to inspect and copy, test, or sample any tangible things that constitute matters within the scope of discovery.

The rules further provide that a party may request that any other party permit the requesting party's entry on designated land or other property for the purpose of inspecting, measuring, surveying, photographing, testing, or sampling the property or a designated object on the property. These requests must be served in writing. The other party must respond in writing either agreeing to the request or objecting.

e. Physical and Mental Examinations.

If the physical or mental condition of a party is in controversy, any other party may request that the court order him or her to submit to a mental or physical examination. The moving party is required to show "good cause" why this examination should be required. Often good cause is apparent from the face of the pleadings, as where the extent of the plaintiff's injuries forms an important area of dispute. If the court orders the physical examination, the party examined is entitled to receive from the discovering party a copy of the written report of the examination.

f. Failure to Make Discovery.

Rule 37 provides that if one party refuses to give the other the discovery that the other requests, the discovering party may ask the court to enter an order compelling discovery. This request is called a motion to compel. The court reviews the request and the other party's objections, then either enters the desired order or denies it.

If the judge grants the motion in whole or in part, he or she may also enter a protective order. Rule 26(c) states that a protective order should be used to shield a party or person from annoyance, embarrassment, oppression, or undue burden or expense. Such an order may require, among other things, that

- certain matters not be inquired into
- discovery should be had only on specified terms and conditions, including a designation of the time or place
- discovery should not be had at all
- only a particular method of discovery may be used
- a deposition should be sealed and only opened by order of the court.

Often a party who files a motion to compel will request the court to order that it should be reimbursed for the expense of preparing and pursuing such a motion. If the court denies the motion to compel, it may instead order the moving party to pay his or her opponent the reasonable expenses that the opponent incurred in opposing the motion. The court should not order either party to pay the expenses of the other if it finds, under the law and the facts and circumstances, that the opponent's failure to give discovery or the discovering party's motion to compel was substantially justified.

5. Motion Practice -- Termination of the Litigation Without Trial.

As discussed in the section on responsive pleadings, a party can obtain dismissal of the case in a number of ways before it has progressed past the filing of a complaint. Two other motions, not previously discussed, that are usually not filed until all pretrial proceedings are complete, also may terminate the case.

The first is a Rule 12(c) **motion for judgment on the pleadings**. Such a motion, which is not appropriate until all pleadings have been filed, is relatively rare. The most common circumstance in which it arises is one in which the defenses raised by the defendant's answer, even if proven, do not relieve the defendant of liability. For example, if a defendant admits the truth of the matters alleged in the complaint but asserts an affirmative defense, the plaintiff may file a motion for judgment on the pleadings in which the plaintiff claims that the affirmative defense is legally insufficient.

A **motion for summary judgment** under Rule 56 is perhaps the most commonly used method of disposing of litigation before trial. Parties use this device when the court records, on their face, show no disputed issue of fact. A motion of summary judgment permits a court to look to evidence beyond the pleadings to determine whether there is any genuine issue of material fact. If there is no such issue, then a trial is unnecessary; the court may simply decide the issues of law and rule in favor of one party or the other.

A party filing a motion for summary judgment submits with the motion any additional evidence that such party wants the court to consider. The evidence might be in the form of deposition excerpts, affidavits in which a witness swears in writing to the truth of a particular fact, or other documentary evidence. The opposing party may then file whatever controverting evidence it wishes the court to consider.

Suppose, for example, that a plaintiff sued a defendant for breach of contract, claiming that a contract between the plaintiff and the defendant required the defendant to deliver to the plaintiff 1000 bushels of corn on or before July 1, that the defendant had only delivered 100 bushels of corn on July 1, and that the plaintiff had suffered damages in the amount of $1.00 per undelivered bushel.

The defendant filed an answer admitting that he had delivered 100 bushels of corn on July 1 but denying that the terms of the contract were as the plaintiff claimed.

The plaintiff then filed a motion for summary judgment, attaching to the motion a contract signed by the plaintiff and the defendant which contract required the defendant to deliver 1000 bushels of corn on July 1 and which set the price of the corn at $2 per bushel. The plaintiff also filed an affidavit in which she swore that, because the defendant failed to deliver the 900 additional bushels of corn, the plaintiff had been forced to buy 900 bushels of corn elsewhere and had paid $3 a bushel for it.

The defendant filed a response in which he merely stated that he did not recall that the contract required him to deliver 1000 bushels.

On the basis of these documents, the court should grant summary judgment in favor of the plaintiff. The plaintiff proved the contract term that defendant's answer had denied and proved, through her sworn and uncontested affidavit, the amount of her damages.

It should be remembered that if there are any contested issues of material fact, a summary judgment motion cannot be granted. Suppose in the preceding example that the defendant's answer had stated that, contrary to the plaintiff's charges, he had in fact delivered 1000 bushels of corn. The plaintiff then filed a motion for summary judgment, attaching an affidavit in which she swore that she had only received 100 bushels. In his response, the defendant filed his own affidavit in which he swore that he had delivered the full 1000 bushels. These conflicting affidavits present a **contested issue of material fact**. The court must deny the motion for summary judgment and have the factual dispute resolved at trial.

A court may grant summary judgment on the entire case or only on certain issues. If the action is an automobile collision case, for example, the court may grant the plaintiff's motion for summary judgment on the issue of negligence and deny it on the issue of damages. The trial will then focus only on the remaining factual question.

Any party to a proceeding may move for summary judgment at any stage in the proceeding after twenty days have elapsed from the filing of the complaint and before trial. In a complex case in which there are numerous allegations, summary judgment is often a useful means of narrowing the issues. In all cases in which there is no genuine dispute as to the facts, such a motion averts an unnecessary trial and saves the court valuable time.

6. The Trial.

In a trial, either a jury or the judge may decide the disputed issues of fact. Rules 38 and 39 provide that any party may request a jury, but if neither party makes such a request, the case is tried to the court. The court, however, in its discretion, may order that the case be tried in whole or in part by a jury.

If the case is to be tried by a jury, after the parties have selected a jury, the attorney for each side makes an **opening statement**. This statement is a brief explanation of that party's position and what that party intends to prove.

The parties then proceed with the presentation of the **evidence**. The plaintiff begins. The plaintiff calls the plaintiff's first witness, who is sworn and then questioned by the plaintiff's attorney. Following this **direct examination**, the defendant's attorney has the opportunity to **cross examine** the witness. Cross examination may be followed by **redirect examination** and **recross examination** until each side has exhausted its questions.

The plaintiff then calls the plaintiff's second witness, and so on, until the plaintiff's attorney decides that he or she has proved a **prima facie case**, that is, the essential elements of the party's claim. The plaintiff's attorney then states that the plaintiff "**rests**" his or her case.

At this time, the defendant's attorney may move for a **directed verdict under Rule 50(a)**. In this motion the defendant's attorney states that the plaintiff did not prove the essential elements of the plaintiff's claim and that the defendant is entitled to judgment.

A directed verdict may be proper in two circumstances. If, for example, the plaintiff had the burden of proving the defendant's negligence but presented no evidence that the defendant was negligent, then the court should grant a directed verdict.

The second circumstance in which a judge may grant a directed verdict is one in which the plaintiff presented on the issue of the defendant's negligence some evidence but so little that reasonable people could not possibly believe that the defendant was negligent.

If the court grants the defendant's motion, the case is withdrawn from the jury, because there remains nothing for the jurors to decide. If the motion is denied, the defendant then presents the defendant's case.

In some federal courts, the defendant's attorney makes his or her opening statement after the plaintiff rests rather than at the beginning of the trial. The defendant's attorney then proceeds to call the defendant's witnesses, examines them, and offers them to the plaintiff's attorney for cross examination. As in the plaintiff's case, the attorneys have the opportunity for redirect and recross examination.

After the defense rests, the plaintiff's attorney may move for a directed verdict. If such motion is denied, the plaintiff may put on **rebuttal evidence** to contradict facts that the defendant introduced. The defendant may then put on his or her own rebuttal evidence, called **rejoinder**. At the end of the evidence, both parties rest.

During the trial, each party's attorney may object to the evidence that the other is about to introduce. When an attorney objects, he or she must state the grounds of his objection. The party who is trying to introduce the evidence will then explain why he or she believes that it is admissible. The judge then applies the complex Federal Rules of Evidence to determine whether admission of the evidence is proper.

When an attorney makes an objection, he or she does so with a dual purpose. First, the attorney wants to keep the evidence out. Second, if the judge admits the evidence, the attorney wants to preserve the right to complain about the erroneous admission of the evidence. The failure of an attorney to object generally waives that party's right to complain on appeal that the evidence should not have been admitted.

At the close of all the evidence, each party again has the opportunity to move for a directed verdict. If the judge does not grant any such motions, the parties then proceed with their **closing arguments**.

Following closing arguments, the judge "**charges**" the jury. In his or her charge, the judge explains the applicable law and the standards of proof that the jurors must use. The judge may, at his or her option, summarize or even comment on the evidence. If the judge comments on the evidence, however, he or she must make clear that the jurors alone are the finders of fact. Because of the danger of prejudicing the jury and thereby forcing a new trial, most federal judges use their power to comment on the evidence only sparingly.

After the jury has been charged, it retires to deliberate. Rule 49 states that a court may require the jury to return with either a **general verdict** or a **special verdict**. If a special verdict is required, the judge submits specific written questions to the jury on each factual issue and asks them to respond in writing.

If the judge instead requests a general verdict, the jury returns with a simple statement either that the jurors find for the defendant or that the jurors find for the plaintiff and award damages in the amount of a certain number of dollars.

If there is no jury, the judge must specify in writing his or her findings of facts and conclusions of law.

7. Motion for Judgment Notwithstanding the Verdict.

Rule 50(b) provides that after the jury has rendered its verdict, the unsuccessful party may request the court to enter in its favor **judgment notwithstanding the verdict**, technically known in rule 50(b) as "judgment as a matter of law." Essentially, the moving party requests the court to set aside the jury verdict and enter judgment in its favor. In order to make this motion, the moving party must have made a motion for directed verdict at the close of the evidence. Such a motion "**j.n.o.v.**" must be made no later than ten days after the court has entered a judgment on the verdict. Rule 50(b) implies that the court should apply the same standard in evaluating a motion for judgment notwithstanding the verdict as it does in reviewing a motion for directed verdict.

8. Motion for a New Trial.

Federal Rule 59(b) permits a dissatisfied party to file with the court a motion for a new trial not later than ten days after the entry of judgment. A judge will grant such a motion if the judge believes that during the course of the trial he or she made a decision that constitutes reversible error or if the judge believes that the jury acted unreasonably or improperly or misunderstood the judge's charge.

9. Judgment.

Rule 58 provides that after the jury has rendered its verdict or the court has decided the case in favor of one party or the other, the court shall enter **judgment** either awarding relief, including the specific amount of damages, or denying relief. The various types of relief that a judgment may grant are discussed in Chapter III.

A judgment has the power of the government behind it. If it awards money damages to the plaintiff and the defendant fails to pay, a sheriff or, upon order of the court, a United States marshal, may execute on (**seize**) the defendant's property to satisfy the judgment. If relief granted is **injunctive** (that is, ordering the defendant not to perform a certain act, or, less frequently, requiring that he or she perform a particular act), then the defendant can be jailed for failing to obey. The entry of final judgment is the last step in a federal district court proceeding.

Personnel of the Federal Courts.

1. The Federal Judge.

The Constitution, which sets forth the method for the selection of federal judges, provides that the President nominates a person to the position and the Senate confirms the person. In practice, the senior U.S. senator of the President's political party from the state where the judge will sit has a powerful voice as to who will be chosen or confirmed. The Senate rarely fails to approve a presidential nominee for federal judge.

This system of political patronage and expediency has resulted in the selection of some outstanding jurists and "many complacent mediocrities."[49] Few qualifications have been established for federal judges. The primary requirement is that they be competent to sit.

Although the law does not require that federal judges must be lawyers, pursuant to 28 U.S.C. §132 this requirement of competency by implication excludes nonlawyers. To help insure that only qualified persons become federal judges, a screening process involving several prominent legal organizations was established to pass on the qualifications of candidates for federal judgeships. This screening process involves both the American Bar Association and the United States Department of Justice.

Once selected, all new federal judges go through a training program, regardless of their legal background. Educational programs, which include orientation seminars for the newly appointed judges, are provided at the Federal Judicial Center. The Federal Judicial Center carries on research activities and conducts training programs not only for federal judges but also for other court personnel.[50] The orientation seminars for the new judges cover federal laws, civil and criminal procedure, sentencing, and court management.[51]

Compensation for federal judges is established by statute. The Constitution provides, however, that federal judges ". . . shall receive for their Services, a Compensation, which shall not be diminished during their Continuance in Office."[52]

The constitutional provision serves a very important purpose: it ensures that if a judge makes a politically unpopular decision, the Congress cannot punish the judge by lowering his or her salary. Thus, if a judge is asked to protect the rights of a disliked minority or individual, he or she can make a decision strictly on the merits of the case, without fearing that, in reprisal, his or her salary will be reduced.

Once nominated and confirmed, federal judges serve for life.[53] They can be removed only through the process of **impeachment** for official misconduct, *i.e.*, on conviction of treason, bribery, or other high crimes or misdemeanors.

This tenure provision of the Constitution does not protect a federal judge from prosecution for a crime that the judge committed during his or her term of office or before taking judicial office.[54] Although conviction of a serious crime or high misdemeanor might not automatically result in the removal of a federal judge from office, such a conviction would probably trigger the impeachment process. It should be noted here, by way of example, that any justice or judge appointed under the authority of the United States who practices law while in office is deemed guilty of a high misdemeanor that would constitute grounds for impeachment.[55]

Impeachment of a federal judge involves the same process that would be used to impeach a President. The House of Representatives would first have to adopt Articles of Impeachment that serve the same purpose as an indictment in ordinary criminal proceedings. Trial on these Articles of Impeachment would then be held in the Senate, with the accused judge having the right to appear on his or her own behalf. A two-thirds vote in favor of impeachment is necessary for a conviction.[56]

As might be expected, the impeachment of a federal judge rarely occurs. Only eleven federal judges have had Articles of Impeachment voted against them by the House of Representatives during the entire history of the federal judiciary. Only seven of those were ultimately convicted by the Senate.[57]

The relative security of federal judges, when compared to the political vulnerability of elected state court judges, has often been the subject of heated debate. Opponents of the federal method of appointment have criticized the federal judiciary as being too isolated from the political process, accusing federal judges of living in "ivory towers" with the thick walls provided by life tenure forming effective barriers to public opinion. Critics have suggested election or shorter terms as methods of making federal judges more sensitive to public opinion. As discussed in Chapter One, however, federal judges need to be autonomous and removed from political pressures in order to make hard but just decisions in difficult situations.

A federal judge is not subject to a mandatory retirement age. When a judge reaches 65, with fifteen years of active service on the bench, or when he or she reaches the age of 70, with at least ten years of active service, the judge may retire.[58] A retired judge often remains very active, however, continuing to discharge the same judicial duties as other judges, although often with a substantially reduced caseload.[59]

2. The United States District Judge and the Judge's Staff.

The first major function of a federal district judge is that of presiding over and ruling on trials. During the progress of a trial, a judge makes numerous decisions (**rulings**) on what evidence should be allowed and what law applies. Not infrequently, a judge finds himself or herself presiding over a case that presents new and previously unresolved issues of law. In such a case, the judge has the challenging responsibility of determining what the law ought to be.

As discussed in Chapter One, a judge who is presiding over a non-jury trial must perform an additional, often difficult task. He or she must take on the role of a jury and decide the facts.

While a judge is hearing one case, as many as three or four hundred cases may be pending that require hearings and rulings. A **docket** is a record of the cases waiting to be tried. Because of the great number of cases on a judge's docket and because new cases are filed daily, a judge must keep all cases moving toward trial or other resolution.

Many judges find that the best way to move their cases is to set deadlines for the lawyers, usually trial dates. Without such deadlines, some cases might not progress at all. A plaintiff's attorney who has a weak case may prefer to keep the case pending indefinitely. Defendants' attorneys normally prefer to delay the trial. Most judges find that if they were to allow cases to remain inactive for long periods of time, their docket would soon become so gigantic that it would be totally unmanageable.

At a 1971 seminar for federal judges, Judge Carter of the U.S. District Court for the Southern District of California[60] discussed the problems inherent in lack of control of the docket. He stated the inevitable results:

> Cases that should be settled or disposed of clog the docket; . . . congestion breeds congestion, and the more the trial calendar becomes crowded or delayed, the less activity there is by lawyers on pending cases, and this congestion leads to further congestion . . . We therefore recommend

> as a matter of principle that calendar control by a court is far superior in the administration of justice, to a system which for all practical purposes, surrenders the control of the calendar to the attorneys who practice in the court.

Feeling the pressure of a trial date, lawyers are sometimes able to work out an amicable settlement. Pretrial and scheduling conferences are set to encourage the parties to meet and discuss the issues and to offer opportunities for settlement. In many courts, parties are strongly encouraged to make a good faith effort to settle their dispute, and settlement discussion are promoted well in advance of any pretrial conference. Methods of alternative dispute resolution such as arbitration, mediation, or summary jury trials are a nonbinding alternative to bringing civil cases to trial. These methods are strongly endorsed by many courts in an attempt to reduce costs and delay.

U.S. Judge Peter T. Fay of Miami, Florida, said:

> All trial lawyers, trial judges and most litigants would undoubtedly agree that a "fair, reasonable settlement" is always the best way to dispose of litigation.

What prevents many cases from settling, of course, is that the parties cannot agree on what is fair and reasonable.

Members of the judge's staff play a major role in helping the judge decide his or her cases and move the docket. These include the **law clerks**, the judge's secretary, the court reporter, and the courtroom deputy. Technically, the latter two are under the supervision of the office of the U.S. District Clerk.

a. Law Clerks.

Law clerks are usually lawyers who have recently graduated from law school at the top of their class. Usually they are employed by the judges for a one or two-year term as assistants to the judges, although it is possible to became a career law clerk.

Law clerks serve at the direction of the judge and perform a broad range of functions that vary from court to court. Frequently, the law clerk's activities center around legal research and writing. He or she engages in discussions with the judge on pending matters and prepares the judge for and attends conferences in chambers with attorneys.

Such law clerks generally perform three other functions: researching motions, drafting memorandum opinions, and preparing jury charges.

As discussed in the previous section, motions are requests of various types submitted to the court for rulings on particular issues. After studying the motion, the response to the motion, and the applicable law, the law clerk may prepare a memorandum for the judge. The judge, based on the law clerk's memorandum, may make a ruling on the motion or request oral argument. If the ruling is complex and involves important legal question, the judge may want to file a **memorandum opinion** that law clerks help the judge prepare. In a memorandum opinion, the judge not only rules for one side or the other but also sets forth in detail the law on which he or she relied in making the decision.

Jury charges, which law clerks may also help prepare, are the written instructions for the jury. They may include one or more specific questions that the jury must answer. These questions are ones of fact around which the resolution of the case revolves.

In a lawsuit over an automobile accident, for example, the jury might be asked: "Do you find that the defendant John Smith drove through the red light at the intersection of 34th and Main Streets?" In answering yes or no to this question, the jury effectively decides the case.

In order for a law clerk to draft a jury charge, he or she not only must be completely familiar with the important facts of that particular case but also must understand the applicable law. Only if the clerk understands the law will he or she be able to ask the relevant questions. For example, the question about running a red light is only pertinent if the law requires a person to stop at a red light.

Some judges do not permit their clerks to draft jury charges. Instead, they prepare the charge themselves, leaving their clerks to perform other tasks.

In addition to legal research, law clerks also perform administrative functions that help the judge keep the docket moving. These clerks serve as the court's contact with the lawyers, working with them to resolve disputes that arise in connection with trial preparation and arranging conferences between the lawyers and the judge. The clerk performing such administrative tasks serves many of the functions of a courtroom deputy, discussed below.

Some judges may prefer their law clerks to perform these jobs, in which case a courtroom deputy performs purely clerical tasks. Other judges choose to allocate all such administrative jobs to their deputy and ask their clerks to work on entirely legal matters.

Most district courts have two law clerks. Case assignments to the law clerks are made in a variety of ways, but most judges assign all even-numbered cases to one clerk and all odd-numbered cases to the other. If a clerk has a preference for a particular subject matter, many judges try to accommodate that preference.

Law clerks must operate under the same high code of conduct as the judge and other members of the judge's staff. Law clerks who have regular contact with attorneys must be impartial and walk a delicate line between being helpful, courteous, and friendly and resisting efforts by lawyers to gain improper advantage or win favors. This balance is sometimes difficult to maintain. For this reason, many courts have delegated the responsibility of dealing with lawyers to the courtroom deputy.

b. Secretary.

In addition to traditional secretarial duties, the judge's secretary handles a wide range of responsibilities to help the judge with public and private matters. The secretary generally types opinions for the judge and the law clerks. If the judge does not use a courtroom deputy for administrative functions, the secretary often shares in the administrative duties by keeping track of the docket and scheduling trials and conferences. In courts where there are as many as 500 cases pending, such a job is extremely demanding.

c. Court Reporter.

The court reporter's responsibility consists of recording all proceedings verbatim by shorthand or by mechanical means and transcribing any proceedings upon the request of a judge or any party to the proceeding. He or she receives a salary from the court and fees from litigants, including the United States, for transcripts requested by them and prepared by the reporter. In many courts, the court reporter also takes responsibility for keeping exhibits introduced during trials.

Court reporters are primarily assigned to a particular judge, although they serve the District court *en banc*. Court reporting services must be available to each judge in all divisional offices.

Under the direction of the District judges, the overall management of court reporters is delegated to the Clerk of Court. The Clerk must:

- equitably apportion the court reporting tasks, known as "pooling"

- assure that the fee charged and format used for all transcripts are in compliance with regulations of the Judicial Conference

- ensure that all transcript preparation is done in a prompt and timely manner and that the quality of transcripts is maintained

- ensure that appeals delivery deadlines are met.

While certification by the state is a requirement for court reporters in most state courts, it is not mandatory for federal court reporters. Unless one is certified, however, one stands little chance of obtaining a position as a federal court reporter. In the past, court reporters experienced a great deal of independence. The Judicial Conference now requires each court to have in place a court reporter management plan that increases supervision and assures the timeliness and quality of transcripts. As a result of this directive, sanctions can be imposed for a case on appeal in which the transcripts have not been delivered within thirty days of the date ordered and paid.

d. Courtroom Deputy.

Formerly, the courtroom deputy's primary function was that of a minute clerk who recorded minutes of courtroom proceedings and had responsibility for marking and keeping exhibits. With the increase in litigation, some judges have found it necessary to delegate administrative and management matters to para-judicial personnel. Many judges have taken the courtroom deputy out of the courtroom and made this individual responsible for managing the court's docket and the court calendar. In fact, the Federal Judicial Center recommends that courtroom deputies be used in this manner.

The courtroom deputy who has calendar responsibility may regulate the movement of cases by fixing dates and times for status conferences and motion hearings. During these conferences the judge may discuss a discovery schedule in the case and a date for trial.

Some cases are not set for trial. For example, social security and bankruptcy reviews are typically decided on the basis of motions. The courtroom deputy may set schedules and follow up on such motions.

Since managing the docket entails a great deal of contact with the attorneys, either by phone or in person, many judges have designated the courtroom deputy as the liaison or contact person for the court in all matters.

In addition to the responsibilities outlined above, the courtroom deputy performs traditional courtroom responsibilities such as administering oaths to jurors, receiving verdicts, and recording minutes of proceedings. In criminal cases, the courtroom deputy may record actions taken during arraignments and sentencing and may prepare appropriate judgments.

3. The United States District Clerk.

The United States district clerk is appointed by and serves at the pleasure of the district judges within a particular judicial District. The clerk's office is the nucleus of the recordkeeping and service function of the courts. All pleadings are filed with, and official records are maintained in, the clerk's office. The size of the clerk's staff varies with the size of the district and the volume of litigation. In metropolitan area courts, the clerk may have as many as 150 deputy clerks. Small division offices may have only one deputy clerk.

The responsibilities of deputy clerks may include:

- receiving and filing new cases and pleadings
- setting up new files
- recording (**docketing**) pleadings on central docket sheets, both paper and automated
- mailing out orders
- assisting the public with locating files
- copying records
- preparing statistical data reflecting the performance of the courts
- receiving, administering, and disbursing court funds
- purchasing supplies
- handling personnel functions.

The summoning of jurors is also handled by the clerk's office. One or more jury clerks are usually assigned the responsibility of administering the jury program. The objective of the program is to make the best use of the jurors' time, while at the same time assuring that the judges have jurors available whenever they are needed. Cases frequently settle at the last minute, sometimes after a jury panel is already in the courtroom. Often it is difficult to predict exactly when jurors may be needed if a judge plans to start a new case immediately after concluding the current one. The jury clerk must thus develop frequent and open communication with the judge's staff.

When a new case is filed in the clerk's office, it is usually randomly assigned to a judge. This method is called the **individual calendar system**. In such a system each judge can become thoroughly familiar with his or her cases and maintain responsibility for the handling of each case from the time that it is filed until the dispute is resolved.

An alternate way of handling cases is the **master or central calendar system**, where several judges may conduct different hearings in one case and no one judge has responsibility for the case.

4. The United States Magistrate Judges.

To help with administrative and judicial functions, judges often look to magistrate judges. The authority of magistrate judges derives primarily from the Federal Magistrates Act of 1968, 28 U.S.C. §636, as interpreted by *Mathews v. Weber*, 423 U.S. 261 (1976).

Magistrate judges are appointed by a majority of the judges of the district court for a term of eight years. They may be removed from office by a majority of the judges for incompetency, misconduct, neglect of duty or physical or mental disability.[61]

To qualify for appointment as a magistrate judge, a person must be under seventy years of age, a member of the Bar in good standing, competent to perform the duties of the office, and unrelated by blood or marriage to a judge of the appointing court. Additional requirements may be imposed by District courts.[62]

Generally, each judge determines which duties a magistrate judge will perform for the judge. Ideally, magistrate judges are given the broadest possible powers within a framework established by judges and within the confines of the law. The Federal Rules for United States Magistrate Judges became effective in May 1969 and prescribe procedures for magistrates judge.[63]

A typical magistrate judge might:

- issue arrest warrants or summonses upon a finding of probable cause in a criminal complaint

- issue search warrants upon a finding of probable cause from the affidavit in support of the application

- conduct preliminary hearings in criminal cases to determine whether there is probable cause to believe that an offense has been committed and that the defendant has committed it

- appoint counsel and set bail and conditions of release under 18 U.S.C. §3146

- serve as special master in civil actions and in habeas corpus proceedings

- assist a district judge in the conduct of civil and criminal pre-trial and discovery proceedings

- where all parties consent, sit as a judge for the trial of cases.[64]

5. The United States Probation Office.

The United States Probation Office is probably best known for its responsibility in supervising persons on probation and parole.

Probation officers perform many other functions as well. They serve at the pleasure of the court and assist the court in criminal matters. Their duties involve preparing pre-sentence investigation reports for use by judges in making sentencing decisions. They also perform investigations and make recommendations to the judges about alleged probation violators.

The sentencing of a defendant is based upon formulas set forth in the Federal Sentencing Guidelines. These guidelines take into consideration the type and seriousness of the offense, contributing circumstances, and the criminal history of the defendant. The guidelines set forth a range with which a judge must sentence the offender. While a judge may depart from the sentencing guidelines when there are aggravating or mitigating circumstances in a particular case, these departures are rare. Reasons for such departures must be specified.

Probation officers also make recommendations to the United States Parole Commission. In this connection, they conduct investigations, make evaluations, and prepare reports concerning parole considerations and recommendations concerning alleged parole violators.

When a defendant requests modification of his or her sentence, the probation officer may assist the court by providing background information and recommendations. Probation officers are often helpful to the judge in preparing responses to the volume of mail that judges receive from prisoners.

6. The United States Marshal.

Deputy United States marshals are sometimes referred to as the police officers of the courts. Although the marshal's office works very closely with the courts, organizationally the marshal's office is part of the executive branch of government rather than the judicial branch. The marshal's office reports to the Attorney General of the United States.

The United States marshal for each district is appointed in a manner similar to that of a federal judge. A candidate is recommended by the senior U.S. senator of the President's political party from the state where the marshal will serve. After a full Senate confirmation, the marshal is appointed to a term of four years, although he or she serves at the pleasure of the President.

In addition to providing security in the courtroom during court proceedings, the marshal is responsible for serving subpoenas, summonses, court orders, writs and, at time, the original complaint. Service of the original complaint is, however, usually made by certified mail or through a private process server. Anyone over eighteen who is not a party to the suit may be a process server.

The marshal's office also has responsibility for transporting and retaining custody of defendants who are appearing in court for arraignment in criminal and, sometimes, in civil cases, for trial or sentencing. In many courts a deputy marshal formally opens and closes court and is present during trial.

In the case of jury trials, the marshal is in charge of the jury and is the only court officer communicating with the jurors outside the courtroom. During a criminal jury trial, several deputy marshals are usually in the courtroom, one in charge of the jury, one to watch the defendant, and one to maintain security in the courtroom in general.

The marshal's office is responsible for protecting the safety of the judge and the judge's staff. This task is an important one. Judges try controversial cases and have the difficult job of sentencing criminal defendants. They often receive threats and need constant, diligent protection.

7. The United States Attorney.

The United States attorney is appointed for a term of four years by the President with the advice and consent of the Senate. The Attorney General of the United States may appoint assistant United States attorneys as needed. Assistant U.S. attorneys can do anything a U.S. attorney can do.[65]

The U.S. attorney's office is a part of the court system only in the sense that the U.S. attorney and assistant U.S. attorneys, like all lawyers, are considered to be officers of the court. Organizationally, the U.S. attorney reports to the Attorney General as head of the Department of Justice.

The Department of Justice is sometimes referred to as the "largest law firm in the nation."[66] It represents the citizens of the United States

> "in enforcing the law in the public interest. The Department also plays a key role in protecting citizens against criminals and subversion, in ensuring healthy competition of business in our free enterprise system, in safeguarding the consumer, and in enforcing drug, immigration, and naturalization laws."[67]

The Justice Department is divided into several major divisions.

With a few exceptions, the Criminal Division is responsible for the enforcement of all federal criminal laws except those specifically assigned to the Antitrust, Civil Rights, and Tax Divisions. The Division has special responsibility for enforcement against organized crime from the initial investigation through the handling of prosecution and appeal. In recent years the number of civil suits filed by inmates of prisons against federal officials have greatly increased. The Criminal Division defends the federal officials named in these actions. The general supervision of laws relating to subversive activities and certain other activities directed against internal security has been transferred to the Criminal Division.[68]

The Antitrust Division is responsible for enforcement of federal antitrust laws. This involves investigating possible antitrust violations, conducting grand jury proceedings, preparing and trying antitrust cases, prosecuting appeals, and negotiating and enforcing final judgments. Such criminal actions arise from alleged restraint on and monopolization of trade. The Consumer Affairs Section of the Antitrust Division is responsible for the institution of civil and criminal proceedings in cases referred to the Department by other agencies such as the Food and Drug Administration and the Federal Trade Commission.

The Civil Rights Division was established in 1957 to secure effective federal enforcement of civil rights laws that prohibit discrimination on the basis of race, sex, color, religion, or national origin. Although litigation in the Civil Rights Division is primarily civil, the Division also enforces specific criminal statutes, including those concerning willful deprivation of constitutional rights while acting under color of law or through conspiracy and violent interference with federally protected activities.[69]

The Tax Division handles litigation arising under the Internal Revenue Code. This litigation may be civil or criminal in nature.

The Civil Division is responsible for representing the United States in civil litigation except certain specialized areas that are assigned to other divisions of the Department. The Civil Division is responsible for "suits and claims on behalf of the government and suits filed against the United States, and actions for injunctive relief and judicial review brought against Cabinet members, the heads of federal agencies, and other government officials."[70]

TERMS TO KNOW

limited jurisdiction
federal question jurisdiction
diversity jurisdiction
diversity of citizenship
exclusive jurisdiction
double jeopardy
pendent jurisdiction
doctrine of judicial self-restraint
justiciable controversy
standing
advisory opinions

receiver
final decision
interlocutory
exclusive
non-exclusive
writ of certiorari
"grants cert"
certificate
original jurisdiction
complaint
denial
discovery
affirmative defense
statute of limitations
answer
motion
motions to dismiss
compulsory counterclaim
permissive counterclaim
settlement
deposition
stipulate
motion to compel
interrogatories
request for admissions
request to produce
motion for judgment on the pleadings
motion for summary judgment
contested issue of material fact
opening statement
evidence
prima facie case
direct examination
cross examination
recross examination
directed verdict under Rule 50(a)
rebuttal evidence
rejoinder
closing arguments
"charges"
general verdict
special verdict
judgment notwithstanding the verdict
judgment
injunctive
impeachment
rulings
docket
law clerks
memorandum opinion
docketing
individual calendar system
master
central calendar system
en banc

FOOTNOTES

1. Mishkin, *The Federal "Question" in the District Courts*, 53 Colum. L. Rev. 157, 168 (1953).
2. C. Wright, *The Law of Federal Courts* 73 (3d ed. 1976).
3. *United States v. Hudson and Goodwin*, 11 U.S. (7 Cranch) 32 (1812).
4. 18 U.S.C.
5. J. Ferguson and D. McHenry, *The American System of Government* 434 (12th ed. 1973).
6. C. Wright, *supra*, at 41.
7. *Id.* at 52
8. *Id.*
9. *Coleman v. Miller*, 307 U.S. 432 (1939).
10. *Luther v. Borden*, 48 U.S. (7 How.) 1 (1849).
11. C. Wright, *supra*, at 38.
12. *Dallas Times Herald*, Sunday Magazine, Nov. 2, 1975.
13. J. Ferguson and D. McHenry, *supra*, at 431.
14. 28 U.S.C. §46.
15. *United States v. Allied Stevedoring Corp.*. 241 F.2d 925, 927 (2d Cir.), *cert. denied*, 353 U.S. 984 (1957).
16. 28 U.S.C. §46.
17. 363 U.S. 685 (1960).
18. C. Wright, *supra*, at 9.
19. 28 U.S.C. §1291.
20. *Catlin v. United States*, 324 U.S. 229 (1945).
21. 28 U.S.C. §1292.
22. 28 U.S.C. §1293.
23. C. Wright, *supra*, at 520.
24. United States Government Printing Office, *The United States Courts* 5 (1975).
25. *United States v. Vida*, 370 F.2d 759 (6th Cir. 1966).
26. *Bauer v. Orser*, 258 F.Supp. 338 (D.N.D. 1966).
27. R. McCloskey, *The American Supreme Court* 4 (1960 ed.)
28. *Id.*
29. R.L. Williams, *The Supreme Court of the United States: the Staff That Keeps Its Operating*. SMITHSONIAN, Jan. 1977, at 41.
30. 28 U.S.C. §1.
31. 28 U.S.C. §2.
32. C. Wright, *supra*, at 527.
33. 28 U.S.C. §1253.
34. 28 U.S.C. §1252.
35. C. Wright, *supra*, at 527.
36. 28 U.S.C. §1252.
37. 28 U.S.C. §1254(2).
38. 28 U.S.C. §1254(3).
39. *United States v. Mayer*, 235 U.S. 55 (1914).
40. 28 U.S.C. §1257(3).
41. C. Wright, *supra*, at 537.
42. U.S. Const. Art. III, §2.
43. 28 U.S.C. §1251.

44. C. Wright, *supra*, at 563.
45. *Ohio v. Wyandotte Chemicals Corp.*, 401 U.S. 493 (1971).
46. C. Wright, *supra*, at 558.
47. 28 U.S.C. §1872.
48. C. Wright, *supra*, at 561.
49. *Dallas Times Herald*, Nov. 15, 1977.
50. *The United States Courts*, *supra*, at 11.
51. E. Pearson, *Federal Judicial Personnel* 1 (1978).
52. U.S. Const. Art. III, §1.
53. *Id.*
54. *United States v. Isaacs*, 493 F.2d 1124 (7th Cir. 1974).
55. 28 U.S.C. §454.
56. J. Ferguson and D. McHenry, *supra*, at 348.
57. *Id.*
58. 28 U.S.C. §371.
59. *In re National Recreation Products, Inc.*, 403 F.Supp. 1399 (C.D. Cal. 1975).
60. Federal Judicial Center, *Seminars for Newly Appointed United States District Judges* (1971).
61. 28 U.S.C. § 631.
62. Federal Judicial Center, *Law Clerk Handbook* (1977).
63. F. Klein, *Federal and State Court Systems -- A Guide* (1976).
64. Federal Judicial Center, *Law Clerk Handbook* (1977).
65. 28 U.S.C. §542.
66. United States Government Printing Office, *United States Government Manual* (1978).
67. *Id.*
68. *Id.*
69. 18 U.S.C. §§241, 242, and 245.
70. United States Government Printing Office, *United States Government Manual* (1978).

CHAPTER VII

CONCLUSION

This book has given you a view of the American legal system much like the view of America which an airline passenger receives by traveling from New York to Los Angeles: the great landmarks are clearly visible, but the intricate byways of each little city or town are too small to be seen with the naked eye.

Like an airplane flight, this condensed approach was necessary if you were to keep your starting point and destination clearly in mind, with some understanding of where you had been in between, and if you were to cover the territory in a reasonable amount of time. There remains much to be seen, and the authors can only hope, now that you know the lay of the land, that you will explore the areas which have piqued your interest at a more leisurely pace, observing firsthand the intricate maze that the law can sometimes be.

Bon voyage!

CHAPTER VIII

GLOSSARY

ABA Code of Professional Responsibility -- Ethical guide promulgated by the American Bar Association

ABA Model Rules of Professional Conduct -- Ethical rules promulgated by the American Bar Association

Abstract of title -- Summary of the transactions by which property has changed hands over the years

Abuse of process -- Malicious prosecution in a civil case

Acceptance -- Receiving a thing offered or tendered by another

Accord and satisfaction -- Method of discharging a contract through compromise between parties disputing the contract

Actual damages -- Damages awarded the victim of a tort, designed to place the tort victim in the place the victim would have occupied had the tort not occurred, to the extent that goal may be reached through a monetary payment

Adeemed legacy -- Legacy destroyed because the specific property in question was destroyed or sold before the testator's death

Adhesion -- A standard contract to which the weaker party must agree if the weaker party wishes to do business with the stronger party

Advance sheets -- Paperback versions of smaller groups of opinions that will later appear in bound volumes

Advisory opinion -- Judicial ruling upon the legality of a government action, whether already accomplished or contemplated, when there is no case or controversy for the court to decide

Adverse possession -- Doctrine under which a party who remains in open, continuous, and adverse possession of a tract of land for a specified amount of time acquires title to the tract of land

Affirmative defense -- Presentation of other pertinent facts that relieve a defendant of liability, even though the defendant may have committed the act with which he or she is charged

Annotation -- A critical or explanatory note

Answer -- Defendant's reply to a complaint

Antitrust Division -- Division of the Justice Department responsible for enforcement of federal antitrust laws

Appeal - Request by a nonsuccessful party that the decision of a lower court be reconsidered by a court of higher authority, such as an appeal from a trial court

Appearance bond -- Bail bond for a minor offense

Arraignment -- Occasion at which the defendant is brought into court and the charge or charges against the defendant are read

Arrest -- Taking an individual into custody

Assault -- Intentional tort; placing another person in apprehension of battery

Assignment of the lease -- Transfer of all of a tenant's interest in property under a lease to a third party

Assumpsit -- Old English writ of an agreement between two citizens from which derived the modern law of contracts

Attractive nuisance -- Condition constituting an unreasonably dangerous condition, which condition might result in injury to children who cannot learn or appreciate the danger

Bail bond -- Legal document containing the promise of a defendant to appear for trial or to forfeit a sum of money

Battery -- Intentional tort; the harmful or offensive touching of another person, including that person's clothing or an object closely associated with that person

Beneficiary -- Third party who benefits from a trust. Also, one who benefits under a will

Bilateral contract -- Contract in which a promise is exchanged for a promise

Bona fide purchaser -- Purchaser who is unaware of any ownership interests not reflected in the deed records

Business tort -- Civil wrong that interferes with the conduct of a person's business. May be created by statute, such as federal securities fraud rules and regulations

Cash bond -- Bail bond for which guarantee is made by a deposit of cash

Causation in fact -- Negligent conduct causing a resulting injury, which injury would not have occurred if the negligent conduct had not occurred

Central calendar system - System of assigning new court cases under which several judges may conduct different hearings in one case with no single judge completely responsible for that case

Certificate *(n.)* -- Document issued by a governmental agency, such as the Secretary of State

Cestui que trust -- Latin term for the beneficiary under a trust; see "beneficiary"

Challenge for cause -- Removing a potential juror for a specific reason

Charges -- See jury charge

Chattel -- Physical object, as opposed to an abstract concept; personal property

Citation -- Order to appear before a judge at a later date

Civil action -- Action by one person against another seeking redress for injury that the first person claims to have suffered

Civil Division -- Division of the Justice Department responsible for representing the United States in civil litigation, except in those certain specialized areas assigned to other divisions of the Justice Department

Civil Rights Division -- Division of the Justice Department responsible for enforcement of civil rights laws that prohibit discrimination on the basis of race, sex, color, religion or national origin

Closing -- Meeting of a buyer and seller during which a purchase and sale is consummated by such actions as the transfer of deeds, mortgages and money

Closing argument -- Counsel's final address to the jury in which counsel summarizes the case, interprets the evidence, and attempts to persuade the jury to reach a desired verdict

Cloud on the title -- Lien or an actual or potential ownership interest by a third party

Commercial paper -- Specialized contract governed by Article 3 of the UCC: promissory notes and drafts

Common law -- Ancient British tradition on which American jurisprudence system is based

Community property state -- One of the fourteen states in which a husband and wife automatically own property jointly

Comparative causation -- Doctrine in strict tort liability under which a defendant's liability may be reduced by a percentage that represents the degree to which the plaintiff's misconduct participated in causing the injury

Comparative negligence -- Theory under which a plaintiff is permitted to recover damages so long as the plaintiff's negligence is not greater than the negligence of the defendant

Compensatory damages -- See "actual damages," above

Complaint -- Charging document that initiates a litigation proceeding; document filed with the court outlining the wrong a plaintiff feels has been done

Compulsory counterclaim -- Defendant's counterclaim arising out of the same transaction or occurrence that is the subject matter of the plaintiff's action

Computer-assisted legal research -- Research conducted electronically through an on-line database rather than in printed volumes

Condemnation -- Proceeding brought by a government agency asking that land be transferred to the government and the current owner paid a fair price therefor

Confidences -- Information protected by attorney-client privilege

Congressional Record -- A verbatim transcript of all proceedings on the floor of the Senate and House

Consideration -- Act that a party performs, or promises to perform, even though he or she has no legal duty to do so, or forbearance, or promise of forbearance, from an act that he or she has a legal right to do

Contested issue of material fact -- Conflicting statements of fact that must be resolved through trial or settlement

Constructive eviction -- Situation in which a landlord so interferes with a tenant's right to possession that the interference is equivalent to a forcible eviction and the tenant is relieved of any further obligations toward the landlord

Contract implied-in-fact -- Contract under which parties have not formally agreed to be bound but have a mutual intent to create a contract, which intent may be inferred from their conduct

Contract implied-in-law -- Contract created by the court when requirements are imposed on a party even though that party has not agreed to be bound by those requirements, so imposed because not to do so would be unfair

Contract of adhesion -- Contract, usually preprinted and standard, to which the weaker party must agree if the weaker party wishes to do business with the stronger party

Contributory negligence -- Theory under which a plaintiff whose own negligence was a contributing cause of his or her injuries can be barred from recovery

Conversion -- Intentional tort; intentional exercise of dominion or control over a chattel that so seriously interferes with the right of another person to control the chattel that the person controlling may justly be required to pay the other person the full value of the chattel

Counterclaim -- Claim filed by a defendant against a plaintiff

Court of limited jurisdiction -- Federal court that may only hear those types of cases that the Constitution empowers them to hear

Court of record -- Court in which the proceedings are recorded by an official or unofficial court reporter (meaning the series of books, not the individual who records the proceedings)

Crime -- Action that offends the morality of society and that society will not tolerate

Criminal action -- Litigation in which the state prosecutes a citizen for breaking laws, as opposed to citizens opposing each other

Criminal Division -- Division of the Justice Department responsible for enforcement of all federal criminal laws except those specifically assigned to the Antitrust, Civil Rights and Tax Divisions

Criminal justice system -- System whereby the federal or a state government brings an action against an individual alleging that the individual has broken a law or laws, thereby committing a crime

Cross-examination -- Questioning of a witness by counsel for the "other side" after a witness has finished direct examination

Curtesy right -- The common law right of a widower to the lands owned by his deceased wife

De novo -- The appeal from a court that is not a court of record, resulting in the re-trying of a case

Deceit -- See "fraud," below

Deed of trust -- Written record evidencing a form of co-ownership created through a mortgage relationship

Deed -- Written record of the transfer of land from one party to another

Defamation -- Tort interfering with the personal rights of another in which one person defames the good name and reputation of a second person

Defective product -- One that does not meet the reasonable expectations of the ordinary consumer as to its safety

Demonstrative legacy -- Gift under a will of a specific sum to be taken from a particular source

Denial -- A defense claiming the plaintiff's claim is untrue

Deposition -- Oral examination, recorded by a court reporter, by any party of any person whom the party believes has relevant information to a matter under litigation

Deterrence -- Objective of a sentence in a criminal matter: stopping a convicted defendant from committing crime in future

Detrimental reliance -- Modern name for "promissory estoppel," below

Devisee -- One who is designated in a will to receive real property

Digest -- Legal research volume in which information is grouped by topic

Direct examination -- Initial questioning of a witness by the prosecutor

Directed verdict -- Motion by a defendant under Rule 50(a) that the plaintiff has not provided the essential elements of plaintiff's claim and, therefore, the defendant is entitled to judgment. Made after plaintiff has rested its case but before defendant presents defendant's case

Disciplinary Rule -- Rule promulgated by a bar association that must be followed by all members

Discovery -- Process of gathering information about a matter prior to trial

Diversity of citizenship actions -- Cases involving a dispute between citizens of different states, or between a state government and a citizen of another state, or between an American citizen and a foreign government, or between an American citizen and a citizen of a foreign country

Diversity jurisdiction -- Case involving disputes between parties who are citizens of different states

Docket -- Central record system of cases ready to be tried

Doctrine of judicial self-restraint -- Doctrine under which federal courts use certain criteria to designate cases for which they refuse to accept jurisdiction

Doctrine of transferred intent -- Theory under which the intent to harm a person is transferred from the intended victim to a second person who is actually harmed

Double jeopardy -- Doctrine under which an individual may not be tried more than once for the same allegation

Dower right -- The common law right of a widow to the lands owned by her deceased husband

Duress -- Severe pressure to force a person to enter into a contract, such as a physical threat or an economic threat

Easement appurtenant -- Implied easement that entitles a party to travel over the land of another party to reach the property conveyed to the first party by the second party

Easement -- Interest in land, less than an estate, which gives one party the right to make some specified use of the land of another party

Ejectment -- Statutory right of a landlord to regain premises and force a tenant to vacate with a minimum of delay

Eminent domain -- A governmental utility may force an owner to sell a tract of land needed for governmental purposes

En banc -- Latin term meaning that all the judges on a court hear a case

Equitable conversion -- Doctrine under which a contract for the sale of property creates not only a legal contractual obligation for the seller to deliver a deed, which in turn delivers the legal title to the property, but also an equitable title to the property that arises on behalf of the buyer as soon as the contract is signed

Equitable ownership -- Status, in addition to legal ownership, created by the doctrine of equitable conversion and or by a trust

Escheat -- Originally, returning of property to the lord of a manor if the deceased person had no heirs; now, returning of property to the state if no heirs can be found

Estate *pur autre vie* -- Estate in land granted to an individual with reference to the lifespan of a second individual

Estate in land -- Category of various ownership interests

Estate tax -- Federal tax imposed on all property remaining in an estate after debts have been paid, together with other property such as certain trust funds and property held in joint tenancy with right of survivorship, less a deduction allowed for property transferred to the decedent's spouse or to charity

Ethical Consideration -- Ethical rule promulgated by a bar association, such as the American Bar Association or a state bar

Evidence -- Documentary or verbal statements and material objects that are admissible in court

Exclusionary rule -- Rule that evidence obtained in violation of standards set out in the Fourth Amendment must be excluded from court

Exclusive jurisdiction -- Specific areas that federal courts have authority to hear

Executive branch -- Branch of the American government containing, on the federal level, the President and the President's appointees in executive departments and, on the state level, the Governor and the Governor's appointees in executive departments

Executor -- Individual named to manage a testator's estate

Exemplary damages -- Compensation to the victim of a tort in a sum designed to punish the tortfeasor and to make an example of the tortfeasor so as to warn others from committing such tort

Exhibit -- Document or other physical object presented in evidence at a trial

Expectation theory -- Concept in contract law that damages should place the injured party in the position he or she would have occupied if the contract had been fully performed

Express contract -- Contract in which parties have expressly agreed, orally or in writing, that each is to be bound to do certain things

Express warranty -- Representation of fact, promises and descriptions made by a seller under the Uniform Commercial Code

Extrinsic fraud -- Fraud wherein the party is aware of the bargain he or she is making but has been induced to make the agreement by a deliberately false representation

False imprisonment -- Intentional tort; restraining a person within a bounded area against that person's will

Federal question jurisdiction -- Jurisdiction of the federal government over certain questions, such as disputes arising under the United States Constitution or treaties made by the United States; as opposed to state jurisdiction

Federal Rules of Evidence -- Rules following by a federal court to determine whether or not evidence is admissible

Federal Rules of Civil Procedure -- Rules promulgated by the federal courts to be followed in civil law disputes

Federal Rules of Criminal Procedure -- Rules promulgated by the federal courts to be followed in criminal law disputes

Federal District Court -- The initial, trial court level of the federal court system

Fee simple -- The most common estate in land, representing complete ownership of the land

Fee simple absolute -- Fee simple estate with maximum possible ownership rights subject to no conditions whatsoever

Fee simple determinable -- Fee simple estate that will expire upon the happening of a specified event

Fee simple subject to a condition subsequent -- Fee simple estate subject to certain conditions

Fee tail -- Estate in land under which land is granted to a male individual and passed to his lineal descendants until such time, if any, as the line of descendants ran out; common in England

Felony -- Major crime for which a severe penalty, such as a substantial fine, imprisonment, or capital punishment, may be assessed

Final decision -- Ends the litigation on the merits and leaves nothing for the court to do but to execute judgment

Fine -- Sentence under which a convicted defendant must pay monetary damages to the government

Forbearance -- The act of refraining from something

Forced heirship statute -- Common law doctrine under which a surviving spouse may elect to take the share, if any, given him or her by the will of the deceased spouse and a share specified in the statute of the state

Forcible entry -- Prohibited entry by a landlord into a tenant's premises; but see "ejectment"

Forcible entry and detainer -- Permits the landlord to regain the premises and force the tenant to vacate with a minimum of delay and legal red tape

Foreclosure -- Seizure and sale of land by a mortgagor to satisfy the debt owed by the mortgagee

Form book -- Book with sample formats of legal documents that may be copied and adapted

Fraud -- Knowingly false representation made to a person upon which that person reasonably relies to his or her detriment in deciding to enter a transaction into which he or she would not otherwise have entered

Fraud in the factum -- See "intrinsic fraud," below

Fraud in the inducement -- See "extrinsic fraud," above

Freehold estate -- Category including the fee simple estate, the fee tail estate, and the life estate

General legacy -- Gift under a will out of the estate in general, as opposed to some specific fund or source

General verdict -- Under Federal Rule 49, a statement by the jury as to the side for which it finds, plaintiff or defendant. Contrast with "special verdict" below

General warranty deed -- Deed including a promise that the grantor holds good title to the property being conveyed

Grand jury -- official body of citizens brought together to decide whether an accused person should be officially charged

Grand jury indictment -- Charge made by an official body of citizens brought together to decide whether a person accused of a crime should be officially charged

Grantee -- One who receives an estate in land entitling that recipient to possession and use of the land

Grantor -- One who gives an estate in land, conveying title to a recipient

Headnotes -- Paragraphs written by editors summarizing important legal points contained in a decision

Heir -- Closest surviving descendant

Holographic will -- Will entirely in the handwriting of the testator and duly signed by the testator

Hung jury -- Jury that is deadlocked and cannot agree on a verdict

Impeachment -- Removal from office of an official, such as a judge, for serious misconduct, such as conviction for a crime

Implied in fact -- contract inferred from conduct

Implied in law -- The law imposes requirements on the parties

Implied warranty of fitness for a particular purpose -- Warranty under the Uniform Commercial Code that the goods being sold are fit for the particular purpose for which the buyer is acquiring the goods and of which the seller is aware

Implied warranty of merchantability -- Warranty under the Uniform Commercial Code that the goods being sold are of average quality, are fit for ordinary purposes, and are adequately contained, packaged and labeled

Implied warranty of title -- Warranty under the Uniform Commercial Code that the goods being sold belong to the seller

Imprisonment -- Sentence for a convicted defendant sending that defendant to prison for a set length of time

Independent administrator -- Executor (see above) who takes charge of a testator's estate without court supervision

Indictment -- Decision by a grand jury that a person must be brought to trial

Individual calendar system -- System of assigning new court cases under which one judge receives the random assignment of a case and handles that case until the dispute is resolved

Indorsement -- Signature of a holder

Injunctions -- A prohibitive writ forbidding a party to do some act

Injunctive -- An order prohibiting a certain act

Intentional infliction of emotional distress -- Intentional tort; conduct so extreme, outrageous, and transcending all bounds of common decency, so as to affect severely another person

***Inter vivos* trust** -- Trust created by a deed

Interference with business relations -- Business tort under which a tortfeasor attempts to interfere with the conduct of another's business affairs

Interlocutory -- Judgment that is not final

Interrogatory -- Series of written questions that one party in a lawsuit submits to another party, which questions must be answered in writing and under oath

Intestate succession -- Distribution of the property of a person who dies without a will

Intrinsic fraud -- Fraud wherein the party is not aware of the nature of the agreement into which he or she is entering

Invasion of privacy -- Tort interfering with personal rights in which the right of quiet enjoyment is denied a person

Investigation -- Initial step in the criminal justice process, generated by observation of a crime, report of a criminal, or belief that a crime is about to occur

Invitee -- One who is on land as a member of the public or to further the business interests of the person owning the land

Irrevocable trust -- Trust that may not be revoked by its maker

Joint tenancy with right of survivorship -- Form of tenancy in common (see below) that provides for automatic passage of the interest of a deceased joint tenant to a surviving joint tenant

Judgment -- Written document containing the decision of a judge. May also mean the amount of damages assessed against a party, as in "obtaining a judgment"

Judgment lien -- Security interest against property of one who loses in a lawsuit held by the one who has prevailed in the suit

Judgment notwithstanding the verdict -- Request to a judge to set aside a jury verdict and enter judgment in favor of the moving party

Judicial branch -- Branch of American government containing the courts

Jurisdiction -- Power or authority of a court to hear and decide a particular kind of case

Jury charge -- Written instructions for the jury, offered by each of the prosecution and the defense

Jury panel -- Group of citizens from whom a jury is selected

Justice Department -- Section of the federal executive branch headed by the Attorney General and responsible for law enforcement

Justiciable controversy -- A matter in which parties and the court grant relief

Law clerk -- As used in this book, a fully-qualified attorney who works for a judge doing research and administrative functions. Also, a student in a law school who works in a law firm during summer months or part-time during the school year

Law journal -- Legal periodical published by a law school

Law review -- Another term for "law journal," above

Leasehold estate -- Estate in land giving one party the use of property but not the title thereto, as opposed to a freehold estate; term of years, periodic tenancy, and tenancy at will

Legal research -- The process of acquiring information on a legal topic

Legatee -- One who is designated in a will to receive personal property

Legislative branch -- Branch of American government containing the elected representatives of the people. On the federal level: Congress. On the state level: the elected legislature

Legislative history -- Record of the passage of a bill through a legislature, beginning with the initial draft

Libel -- Tort of written defamation

License -- In real property law, a limited right to use land for a specific purpose; not an estate interest

Licensee -- With respect to torts, a visitor on land for a legitimate purpose and with permission of the landowner, but not as an ordinary member of the public or for a business purpose of the landowner

Lien -- Security interest

Life estate -- Estate in land granted to an individual for the duration of that individual's lifetime

Limited jurisdiction -- Courts that may only hear cases the Constitution empowers them to hear

Livery of seisin -- Medieval term denoting transferring land by the parties going to the land and the grantor's giving the grantee a clod of earth or twig to symbolize transfer of the land

Malicious prosecution -- Tort interfering with personal rights under which one person seeks to bring another, innocent person to trial

Master -- In agency theory, one who authorizes another to act in his or her place

Master calendar system -- See "central calendar system" above

Materialmen's lien -- Lien (see above) in favor of suppliers of construction materials

Mechanic's lien -- Lien (see above) in favor of contractors or workmen

Memorandum opinion -- Detailed ruling by a judge containing not only a decision but also specifics of the law on which the judge relied for his or her decision. Initially prepared for the judge by a law clerk

Miranda warning -- Verbal admonition advising a person under arrest of the rights he or she has under the United States constitution, such as the right against self-incrimination and the right to have an attorney present

Misdemeanor -- Minor crime, varying from a traffic violation to theft of a small amount of money

Mistrial -- Declaration by a judge that the trial may not go forward, possibly because of a hung jury, and that the defendant must be tried again

Mortgage -- Deed of trust; a lien on or interest in land arising from the consent of the owner

Mortgagee -- Owner of the interest in land

Mortgagor -- Holder of the property who pays the mortgagee to reside on the land in which the mortgagee has an interest

Motion -- Request submitted to the court for a ruling on a particular issue or issues; request that a court act in a certain manner

Motion for change of venue -- Request to have the trial held in another geographical site, invoked when the defense counsel alleges that the defendant cannot receive a fair trial at the original venue due to pre-trial publicity or some other cause

Motion for judgment on the pleadings -- Motion under Rule 12(c), not appropriate until all pleadings in a matter have been filed with the court. Filed by plaintiff claiming that defendant's answers are not sufficient to relieve defendant of liability. Relatively rare

Motion for summary judgment -- Motion under Rule 56 asking the court to look to evidence beyond the pleadings filed and determine whether there is any genuine issue of material fact. If none is found, the court may decide the issues of law and rule in favor of one party or another without the matter going to trial. Appropriate when both plaintiff and defendant agree on issues of material fact

Motion to compel -- Motion under Rule 37 under which one party asks the court to order the other party to respond to the discovery requests filed by the first party

Motion to dismiss -- Request that the charge against a defendant be dismissed

Motion to sever -- When two or more defendants are accused of the same crime, motion to try each defendant separately

Motion to suppress evidence or to dismiss the indictment -- Defense motion claiming that the grounds of the charge are not sufficiently specific or that the evidence against the defendant was obtained illegally

Negligence -- Tort consisting of four basic elements: a duty to conform to a certain standard established by law, a failure to meet such standard, a cause-and-effect relationship between that failure and the resulting injury, and damages resulting from the injury

Negligence per se -- violation of a statute prohibiting certain conduct, which statute was enacted to benefit a class of persons

Negligent misrepresentation -- Business tort under which one person misleads another to induce the second person to enter into a business transaction

Negotiable -- Transferable; may be assigned non-subject to defenses of which the transferee was unaware when the transferee accepted the negotiable instrument

Negotiable instrument -- Note or draft that may be negotiated from one owner to another by indorsement

Nolo contendere -- "I will not contest it," an alternate plea to "guilty" or "not guilty"

Nominal damages -- Damages awarded the tort victim when such victim has suffered no loss; damages in a very small sum, such as $1

Non-exclusive jurisdiction -- Jurisdiction by either a federal or a state court, not reserved exclusively to the federal court

Nonconforming use -- Use of land that is inconsistent with the land's zoning classification, permitted to remain on the land because the use was in existence at the time such zoning classification was enacted, with the proviso that such use may not be changed or expanded

Novation -- Agreement between parties to a contract that a third party will assume some or all of the contractual obligations of one of the original parties

Nuisance -- Label given to a variety of torts that are deemed either private or public nuisances

Nuisance per se -- nuisance under all circumstances

Nuncupative will -- Will made by speaking

Offer -- Communication by one party to another party that reasonably leads the receiving party to believe that the offering party is willing to enter into a contract

Official reporter -- Reporter published by a government agency

"One-bite" rule -- The owner of a cat or dog is not liable on the first occasion to which a pet bites a person

Opening statement -- Brief statement of a party's position and what the party intends to prove at trial

Original jurisdiction -- Jurisdiction under which a matter is first tried

Parol evidence rule -- rule under which statements, either oral or written, but usually oral, outside a written contract may not be used to contradict the terms of the contract

Partition -- Division of land demanded by a tenant in common so that such tenant in common will receive exclusive title of a portion of the land, such portion representing the tenant in common's fair share

Pendent jurisdiction -- The federal district court may make decisions on matters that would otherwise be exclusively heard by the state court

Per capita -- System of distribution of property in an estate whereby each person entitled to a share of the estate takes an equal share

Per stirpes -- System of distribution of property in an estate whereby each descendant of the testator takes a share representing a proportionate distribution of the property at each succeeding generation

Peremptory challenge -- Removing a potential juror without any stated reason

Periodic tenancy -- Leasehold estate existing for a given period of time and automatically renewing itself unless one party notifies the other party that renewal is not desired

Permissive counterclaim -- Defendant's counterclaim arising out of an incident other than the one that is the subject matter of the plaintiff's action

Personal recognizance -- Promise of defendant to appear at trial, without a sum of money to guarantee such appearance. See "bail bond," above

Plea bargaining -- Negotiation between the prosecutor and defense counsel to have the defendant enter a guilty plea in exchange for some benefit to the defendant, such as a reduction of charges against the defendant

Pocket part -- Annual supplement fitted into the back of a volume containing statutes, keeping the volume current as statutes are amended

Precedent -- Same as *stare decisis*

Presentence report -- Report compiled by a federal probation officer, summarizing an investigation of the background of a defendant who has been found guilty and recommending a sentence

Pretermitted child statute -- Statute that revokes a will if the testator had no living children at the time of making of the will but later had a child who survived the testator by at least one year

Pretrial release program -- Program under which a defendant is allowed release until trial in return for paying a small premium on a bail bond called a pretrial release bond. See "bail bond"

Prima facie case -- The essential elements of a party's claim

Primary source -- Information from a direct source of law, such as a court opinion

Private nuisance -- Interference with a landowner's right to possession and enjoyment of the landowner's land

Privilege against self-incrimination -- Privilege, provided by a clause in the Fifth Amendment of the Bill of Rights, that one shall not be compelled to be a witness against oneself

Probable cause -- evidence that leads a reasonable person to believe that guilt is more than a possibility

Pro bono publico -- "For the good of the public"

Probate -- Presentation of a will to the probate court for public filing

Probation -- Sentence under which a convicted person is not imprisoned but must report to a probation officer

Probation revocation hearing -- Hearing at which the convicted defendant on probation is called before the court to determine if such probation should be revoked

Procedural due process -- Rights and privileges available under the Bill of Rights to the defendant in a criminal matter

Procedure -- Step-by-step mechanics that people bringing or defending a lawsuit or criminal prosecution must follow

Production of documents -- Discovery request pursuant to Federal Rule 34, by which a party to a lawsuit may be requested to produce, and to permit the other party to inspect and copy, any designated documents

Products liability -- Strict liability tort involving products that are defective and unreasonably dangerous

Profits or *profits a prendre* -- Right to sever minerals or crops from land; not an estate interest

Promissory estoppel -- Doctrine under which a promise by a promising party should reasonably expect to cause, and that indeed does cause, definite and substantial reliance by the other party and, therefore, requires no consideration

Promissory note -- Type of commercial paper evidencing a maker's promise to pay to the order of a lender principal and interest at a future date

Protection of the public -- Objective of a sentence in a criminal matter: shielding the public from actions of a convicted defendant

Protective order -- Under Rule 26(c), order by the court to shield a party from annoyance, embarrassment, oppression, or undue burden or expense

Proximate causation -- Concept in tort liability under which injuries result, although not directly, from an action or failure to act

Public defender -- Office of attorneys who defend accused persons who cannot afford representation

Public nuisance -- Interference with the rights of the public generally

Punitive damages -- See "exemplary damages," above

Quasi-contract liability -- Liability resulting from a contract implied in law

Quiet enjoyment -- Possession of real property without interference

Quitclaim deed -- Deed containing no warranties, giving the grantee whatever interest in the property, if any, that his or her grantor had at the time of the deed

Rebuttal evidence -- Opposing evidence or arguments

Receiver -- Neutral party appointed by the court to preserve property during the course of litigation

Recross examination -- Questions of a witness by counsel for the "other side" for a second time

Regional reporter -- Reporter dealing with published judicial opinions in a stated geographic area

Rehabilitation -- Objective of a sentence in a criminal matter: changing the life style of a convicted defendant so that defendant may return to society

Rejoinder -- Rebuttal evidence by a defendant

Remainder -- Portion of an interest in property held not by the grantor or grantee but by a third party

Reporter -- Volume of published judicial opinions

Request for admissions -- Request from a party to a lawsuit that opposing party admit or deny the truth of matters within the scope of discovery that relate to statements, opinions of fact, or the application of law to fact

Request to produce -- Request by a party in a lawsuit to inspect and copy any designated documents

Res ipsa loquitur -- "The thing speaks for itself"

Rescission -- Discharge of a contract ordered by a court under which the contract is declared void and each party returns to the other party or parties any benefits received under the contract

Residuary legacy -- Gift under a will of the balance of the testator's estate after all debts and other legacies have been paid

Restitution -- In criminal law, a sentence under which a convicted defendant must pay monetary damages to the defendant's victim. In tort law, the concept of restoring a party to the position he or she would have occupied if the tort had not occurred

Restrictive covenant -- Restriction in a deed limiting the use to which land may be put or the individuals to whom the land may be conveyed; not an estate interest

Retribution -- Objective of a sentence in a criminal matter: punishing a convicted defendant

Reversion -- Portion of an interest in property still held by the grantor

Revocable trust -- Trust that may be revoked by its maker

Right of eminent domain -- Right to unfettered use and possession of land

Right of survivorship -- Upon the death of one joint tenant, that tenant's interest automatically passes to the other joint tenant(s)

Right of way easement -- Specified use of land for passing over another's land to reach his or her own property

Rule against perpetuities -- Common law rule under which an instrument, such as a trust, establishes a time limit beyond which no interest may vest under the instrument

Rules of procedure -- Step-by-step rules to be followed when bringing a matter before a court

Rulings -- Court decisions on what evidence should be allowed and what law applies

Secondary source -- Source of legal research not stemming from government, such as a legal treatise or a law review (see above)

Secrets -- Information that the client has requested to be kept secret because it could be embarrassing or detrimental to the client

Secured transaction -- Sale of goods covered by Article 9 of the Uniform Commercial Code under which one party obtains a security interest in goods or other personal property owned by another party

Security interest -- Same as lien or mortgage

Self-proving affidavit -- Affidavit attached to a will executed by the testator and two witnesses before a notary, which by its very existence attests to the proper execution of the will

Sentence -- Punishment set by a judge for a convicted defendant

Sentencing guideline -- Part of the Federal Criminal Code setting the minimum and maximum sentence that may be assessed for conviction in a federal court

Session law -- The text of a statute and amendments thereto, written precisely as they were enacted at a given session of the legislature that passed the law

Settlement -- Resolution of dispute without trial

Settlor -- One who makes a trust. See "trustor" below

Shepardizing -- Using *Shepard's Citations* to establish if a reported case has been followed by a lower court as precedent or overturned by a higher court; determining if a ruling is still "good law"

Slander -- Tort of verbal defamation

Slip law -- Recently enacted statute printed individually in booklet form

Slip opinion -- Recently issued opinion printed in booklet form

Special verdict -- Under Federal Rule 49, a verdict in which the jury responds in writing to specific written questions on factual issues. Contrast with "general verdict" above

Special warranty deed -- Deed promising only that the grantor is giving the grantee as good a title as the grantor originally received from his or her grantor, further promising that the grantor has done nothing to impair the title to the property during the grantor's ownership of it

Specialized reporter -- Volume of court decisions on a particular area of the law, such as securities or bankruptcy

Specific devise -- Testamentary gift of a specific tract of land

Specific legacy -- Testamentary gift of a specific object

Specific performance -- Performance ordered by the court of a party found guilty of breach of a contract

Split sentence -- Combination of imprisonment followed by probation

Standing -- Personal stake in litigation of a sufficient nature to justify bringing suit, as a person must show "standing" in a federal court

Stare decisis -- Principle that when a court has decided a case based upon a set of facts, that decision provides guidance for other courts faced with similar sets of facts

Statute -- Prohibition, command, or declaration enacted by a legislative body

Statute of Frauds -- 1677 English statute that has been adopted through the United States requiring certain types of contracts to be in writing

Statute of limitations -- Term during which plaintiff may sue

Stipulate -- To agree

Strict liability tort -- Civil wrong for which a person may be held liable despite having acted with the utmost care

Sublease -- Transfer by a lessee of less than all rights under a lease, making a tenant a "junior landlord" to whom the sublessee owes obligations as a tenant

Substantive Law -- Legislative enactments or decisions handed down by judges

Surety bond -- Bail bond by which guarantee is made by a second person's promise to pay if the defendant fails to appear for trial

Suspended sentence -- Sentence under which a convicted defendant may stay in society under probation and under which, should the defendant violate terms of the probation, the defendant goes immediately to prison for a set amount of time

Tax Division -- Division of the Justice Department responsible for litigation arising under the Internal Revenue Code, either civil or criminal

Tax lien -- Security interest arising from unpaid taxes

Tenancy at will -- Leasehold estate terminable without advance notice by either party

Tenancy by the entireties -- Specialized form of joint tenancy between husband and wife

Tenancy in common -- Means by which two or more persons may concurrently own a single piece of land under which each has an undivided interest in the land

Term of years -- Leasehold estate giving a grantee the right to possession and use of real property for a specified period of time; a fixed-term lease

Testamentary trust -- Trust created within a will

Testator -- One who makes a will

Title insurance -- Policy under which an insurance company will make good losses to buyer if, at a later date, it is discovered that a defect exists in title to a property

Title opinion -- opinion of an title company stating that, based on its research, the seller holds good title to property

Title search -- Tracing a chain of grantors and grantees of a property

Tort -- Act, or omission to act, that causes legal harm to another, committed under circumstances where the law imposes a duty to refrain from causing such harm

Tortfeasor -- One who commits a tort

Transferred intent -- Doctrine in tort law wherein the intent to harm one person is transferred to the person who was actually harmed

Treatise -- Legal reference book written by a law professor or other legal scholar

Trespass -- Intentional tort; interference with a person's right to exclusive and complete possession of land or tangible goods

Trespasser -- One who is on land without express or implied permission of the landowner

Trust -- Transaction developed by the courts of equity whereby a trustor conveys title to a trustee for the benefit of a beneficiary

Trustee -- One to whom the legal title to real or personal property is conveyed in a trust transaction so that trustee may hold such title for the benefit of a third party

Trustor -- Maker of a trust, also called the settlor; the one who conveys legal title to the trustee in a trust transaction

Undue influence -- Severe pressure of a moral nature that forces a person to enter into a contract he or she would otherwise have avoided

Unfair competition -- Business tort under which one person used unlawful means to compete with another in a business setting

Uniform Commercial Code -- Model law setting up uniform priorities for commerce such as the sale of goods, secured interests, and negotiable instruments

Uniform Simultaneous Death Act -- When testator and beneficiary die almost simultaneously, half the property passes as though testator had died first, and half as though the beneficiary had died first

Unilateral contract -- Contract that contemplates actual performance as the form of acceptance

United States Attorney -- Attorney appointed by the President with the advice and consent of the Senate for a term of four years, reporting to the Attorney General

United States Court of Appeals -- Federal court of higher jurisdiction to which cases from a federal district court may be appealed

United States District Clerk -- Supervisor of the record-keeping and service functions of a federal district court

United States Magistrate -- Attorney appointed to assist a federal judge with administrative and judicial functions

United States Marshal -- Law enforcement officer in the executive branch of federal government, reporting to the Attorney General

United States Probation Office -- Section of the federal court system responsible for supervising persons or probation and parole

United States Supreme Court -- Highest court of the United States; representative of the third branch of the division of powers between judicial, executive and legislative branches

Unjust enrichment -- Doctrine under which one party unfairly receives a benefit not intended

Unofficial reporter -- Volumes of reported cases published by a private legal publishing company; in general use because the unofficial reporters appear much sooner than the official reporters published by the government

Utility Easement -- Specified use of land for utilities

Vendor's lien -- Lien in favor of the seller of property to insure that the seller receives the full purchase price

Venue -- Geographical location of a matter; site at which a case is being tried

Verdict -- Decision of the triers of fact: the jury

Voir dire examination -- Examination of potential jurors

Widow's election will -- Will giving the surviving spouse of a testator the option to take what the will gives the spouse or, alternatively, to take his or her own half share of the community property, irrespective of the provisions of the will

Writ of assumpsit -- Virtually no contract liability can be created except by agreement

Writ of certiorari -- Petition of a party that a ruling made in the Court of Appeals be heard again and reviewed by the Supreme Court

Writ of trespass -- In medieval times, a quasi-criminal remedy for redress of a direct and usually intentional injury

Zoning ordinance -- Local laws by which a city regulates the use to which land may be put and structures that may be erected upon the land

INDEX